Jesus' Baptism
and
Jesus'
Healing

Jesus' Baptism and Jesus' Healing

His Personal Practice of Spirituality

BRUCE CHILTON

TRINITY PRESS INTERNATIONAL
Harrisburg, Pennsylvania

Trinity Press International, P.O. Box 1321, Harrisburg, PA 17105
Trinity Press International is a division of the Morehouse Group

Library of Congress Cataloging-in-Publication Data

Chilton, Bruce.
    Jesus' baptism and Jesus' healing : his personal practice of spirituality / Bruce Chilton.
       p.   cm.
    Includes bibliographical references and index.
    ISBN 1-56338-248-2 (pbk. : alk. paper)
    1. Jesus Christ – Baptism. 2. John, the Baptist, Saint.
3. Baptism – History.   I. Title.
BT350.C48   1998
232.9'5 – dc21   98-39833

Printed in the United States of America

98 99 00 01 02   10 9 8 7 6 5 4 3 2 1

Contents

Preface

Jesus has been rediscovered as a historical figure in recent scholarship, and that marks an intellectual revolution. After all, it was fashionable thirty years ago to assert (despite overwhelming evidence to the contrary) that Jesus never existed. But although the return of Jesus to historical consideration is only to the good, some of the attention he has received has been peculiar. If the Jesus of today's fashion in North America is Jewish, that is in name only. For John Dominic Crossan, he is at base a cosmopolitan Cynic; for Marcus Borg, he is a generic holy man.[1] For neither of them is Jesus truly a product of Judaism.

In previous works, I have shown that Jesus cannot be assessed except within his Judaic milieu. His preaching of the kingdom of God took up the actual vocabulary of the Aramaic translation of the book of Isaiah (the Targum), which was current in an oral form within the synagogues of his time.[2] In much of his characteristic

---

1. For a full discussion, see Bruce Chilton, "Jesus within Judaism," in *Judaism in Late Antiquity*, part 2: *Historical Syntheses*, Handbuch der Orientalistik 17, ed. J. Neusner (Leiden: Brill, 1995) 262–84.

2. See Bruce Chilton, *God in Strength: Jesus' Announcement of*

teaching, the phrasing of that Aramaic Targum shines
through the Greek text of the Gospels as we can read
it today.[3] The influence of Galilean Judaism is not only
evident in Jesus' words, but in his deeds: by occupying
the Temple in order to insist upon his own view of purity, Jesus courted his own execution.[4] Indeed, his entire
preaching of the kingdom is to be seen in the context
of a quest for the purity God demands as king, a quest
which finds a language of expression in the book of
Psalms.[5]

One of the great fears which comes into play in the
historical study of Jesus is religious: if we locate him in
Judaism, does that involve giving up a Christian spirituality? I understand that fear, but in my experience
the result of critical work is just the opposite. Jesus' Judaism involved an emphatic discipline of spirituality. In
Jesus' Prayer and Jesus' Eucharist,[6] I have already shown

---

the Kingdom, Studien zum Neuen Testament und seiner Umwelt 1
(Freistadt: Plöchl, 1979); reprinted in *The Biblical Seminar* (Sheffield:
JSOT, 1987).

3. See Bruce Chilton, *A Galilean Rabbi and His Bible: Jesus' Use
of the Interpreted Scripture of His Time* (Wilmington: Glazier, 1984);
also published with the subtitle *Jesus' Own Interpretation of Isaiah*
(London: SPCK, 1984).

4. See Bruce Chilton, *The Temple of Jesus: His Sacrificial Program
within a Cultural History of Sacrifice* (University Park: Pennsylvania
State University Press, 1992).

5. See Bruce Chilton, *Pure Kingdom: Jesus' Vision of God*, Studying the Historical Jesus 1 (Grand Rapids: Eerdmans; London: SPCK,
1996).

6. Bruce Chilton, *Jesus' Prayer and Jesus' Eucharist: His Personal*

how Jesus' Aramaic model of prayer and his development of fellowship in meals provided definite examples, commended for emulation and further development among those who follow him. Spirituality is not just an intellectual exercise; it is a communal and practical matter. That is one of the principal results of appreciating Jesus within a Judaic context.

So here we take a big step further into the spirituality of Jesus. Because Judaism was concerned with humanity as pure before God, prepared in a state to be compatible with divine holiness, Jesus could not and did not ignore the issue of purity. *Jesus' Prayer and Jesus' Eucharist* has already shown that in regard to fellowship in meals. Now we turn to the practice of immersion (baptism), one of the more characteristic elements of Judaism in the time of Jesus.

That means we must understand John the Baptist in his relationship to Jesus. To accomplish that, in chapter 1, we will focus on the Judaic sense of John's (or, as we shall learn to call him, Yohanan's) activity, paying especial attention to the evidence of Josephus. Josephus will also guide us in chapter 2, when we consider how politically sensitive Yohanan's activity and that of Jesus (Yeshua) was. Between Yohanan and Yeshua there lies a revolution in the understanding of purity: what Yohanan thought of as being prepared for purity, Yehsua claimed was already pure, and on the cusp of God's

---

Practice of Spirituality (Valley Forge, Pa.: Trinity Press International, 1997).

kingdom. In that revolution we discover the wellspring of the distinctively Christian teaching of the renewed activity of God's spirit. As he drew the lines of purity afresh within his practice, Yeshua also restored to fellowship in Israel those seen to be beyond society, in the realm of the unclean: his radical practice of inclusive purity included the power to heal (chapter 3). Finally, the experience of the church after the resurrection, especially in the circle of Peter, found in baptism in Jesus' name the occasion when that same spirit which had been active in Jesus became available to those who believed with its full healing power (chapter 4).

Dr. Harold W. Rast of Trinity Press International has provided me the occasion and the encouragement to investigate Jesus' spiritual practice, which has not been a topic of critical inquiry until now. I am grateful to him, as I am for the opportunity to serve as the Igor Kaplan Lecturer in Jewish Studies at Toronto University, where some of the material presented here was first developed. Michael Steinhauser, John Kloppenborg, and Andrew Lincoln and his wife, Carol, were all charming hosts and helpful partners in conversation.

Yohanan the Purifier

The Problem of Apologetics in Dealing with "John the Baptist"

There is a remarkable romanticism in the figure of John the Baptist. He is a pivotal figure within the Gospels, and the Gospels largely form the basis on which many people conceive of religious figures. The Gospel according to Mark is the earliest Gospel, and it makes the place of John plain in its proclamation (Mark 1:1–8):

¹ Beginning: the message of Messiah Yeshua, God's son, ² just as is written in Yesaias the prophet:

> Look, I send my messenger before your face who will prepare your way. ³ Voice of one calling in the wilderness — Prepare the Lord's way, make his paths straight.

⁴ Yohanan the immerser was in the wilderness, preaching an immersion of repentance for the release of sins. ⁵ And there came out to him all the Jewish land and all the Yerusalemites, and they

were immersed by him in the river Jordan while
confessing their sins. [6]And Yohanan was clothed in
camel's hair, a skin strap around his hips, and he
ate locusts and field-honey. [7]He preached:

> One who is stronger than I comes after me,
> before whom I am not worthy to bend down
> and loosen the tie of his sandals. [8]I immerse
> you in water, but he will immerse you in holy
> spirit.

This translation will seem both familiar and strange. Familiar, because it takes up material which is well known, not only from Mark, but from its repetition in Matthew and Luke. But strange, because the translation departs from usual conventions, reflecting how the beginning of Mark would have been heard by Greek-speakers in the first century. When we attend to that, the boldness of the Christian claim about John becomes more obvious: Yohanan, a practitioner of purity by immersion in water in "the Jewish land," is turned into the prophet of Messiah Yeshua. Or, to put the matter in our received language, John the Baptist is the herald of Jesus Christ.

Walter Wink has expressed that tradition very accurately in an influential study: Yohanan became "the frontier character of the Christian proclamation."[1] But there is a certain irony here. What Wink says is precisely

---

1. Walter Wink, *John the Baptist in the Gospel Tradition*, Society of New Testament Studies Monograph Series 7 (Cambridge: Cambridge University Press, 1968), 113.

to the point, because he speaks of "Christian proclamation": he understands that, as presented in the Gospels, Yohanan is an apologetic figure. Indeed, that is implicit in the statement attributed to Yohanan in Mark 1:8: "I immerse you in water, but he will immerse you in holy spirit." That promise was not fulfilled within the historical program of Jesus, because Jesus is not reported in the Synoptic Gospels to have baptized people in water or in spirit. But within the experience of the church, where the holy spirit was held to guide the leadership (see Acts 2) and to be personally available to every Christian in baptism (see Acts 10), these words in Mark become a program of action. Indeed, Mark's Gospel proceeds to relate the immersion of Yeshua by Yohanan, because that experience was the archetype of Christian initiation.

Here, as elsewhere, it is all too easy to confuse the faith of the first Christians with assertions of historical fact. That is what brings us to the irony just referred to. Scholars have been famously skeptical about Yeshua, but there is still a widespread willingness to embrace the picture of Yohanan as a prophet of Yeshua. It is said in the source of Yeshua's sayings known as "Q" (which I have described as a mishnah of Yeshua's teaching[2]) that he compared Yohanan with the messenger referred to in the book of Malachi (see Matt. 11:7–19; Luke 7:24–35). That shows how deep the evaluation of Yohanan as

---

2. See Bruce Chilton, *Pure Kingdom: Jesus' Vision of God,* Studying the Historical Jesus 1 (Eerdmans: Grand Rapids, 1996), 60–62, 129–30.

Yeshua's herald is, but the irony is that while scholarship is duly skeptical about whether Yeshua ever said such a thing, there is a willingness to accept that Yohanan really was such a figure.

The same romanticism which makes Yohanan a more vivid figure than Yeshua in Rembrandt's paintings and *The Last Temptation of Christ* (whether the book by Kazantzakis or the film by Scorcese) also gives scholars too much optimism that they understand Yohanan. After all, no extant source from his own movement attests Yohanan's actual character or motivation. So, for example, scholars otherwise at odds with one another, like Robert Webb and E. P. Sanders, accept that Yohanan was a prophet of eschatological repentance who prepared the way for Yeshua.[3] But if the reference to Yohanan in the Gospels is to show the way to Yeshua, both to the eye of faith and in the practice of baptism in the name of Yeshua, then the Gospels are not a suitable point of departure for a critical understanding of Yohanan.

Fortunately, Josephus also portrays Yohanan and the impact of his activity. He takes the story up from the time that Aretas defeated Herod Antipas in a military

---

3. E. P. Sanders, *Jesus and Judaism* (Philadelphia: Fortress, 1985); Robert L. Webb, *John the Baptist and Prophet: A Socio-historical Study,* Journal for the Study of the New Testament Supplement 62 (Sheffield: Sheffield Academic Press, 1991). See the discussion of these and other contributions in Bruce Chilton, "John the Purifier," *Judaic Approaches to the Gospels,* International Studies in Formative Christianity and Judaism 2 (Atlanta: Scholars Press, 1994), 1–31.

dispute about boundaries. He reports that some in Israel saw the destruction of Herod's army as God's recompense for Herod's execution of Yohanan. He then goes on briefly to describe Yohanan's activity:

> For indeed, Herod killed this good man, who also commanded to come together in immersion those Jews who were dedicated to virtue and practiced righteousness towards one another and reverence towards God. For so indeed it seemed to him necessary that bathing be, not for whatever sins they practiced, but for sanctification of the body, with the soul indeed also already cleansed by righteousness. (*Antiquities* 18 §117)

Here, of course, there is no mention of Yeshua, although Josephus mentions him elsewhere (*Antiquities* 18 §§63–64).[4] Yohanan appears in his own right, and the sense of his program is straightforward as Josephus explains it. To some extent, of course, Josephus simply portrays Yohanan as a good Jew: the emphasis on righteousness and reverence is often cited as the content of Judaism throughout Josephus's work.[5]

---

4. Steve Mason remarks, "It is a mark of Josephus' complete isolation from the early Christian world of thought that he devotes significantly more space to John the Baptist than to Jesus — even if we admit his account of Jesus as it stands (but see below)"; *Josephus and the New Testament* 1 (Peabody, Mass.: Hendrickson, 1992), 151. "Complete" would seem to be an exaggeration, but the point he is trying to make stands.

5. So ibid., 153.

Josephus portrays Yohanan as focused on how an Israelite might be pure, acceptable to God. In his description, there is a two-stage process. First, one's "soul" (*psukhe*) was to be "cleansed" (a form of the verb *katharo*) by righteousness, and then one's body was by immersion to be placed in a state of sanctification (*hagneia*). There is no reason to doubt that Josephus correctly conveys the intent of Yohanan's activity: purity is the obvious purpose of immersion within any form of ancient Judaism which is known. But there is every reason to be cautious about Josephus's account of the theology of Yohanan's immersion.

Josephus's Tendentious Presentation of Yohanan

We after all know Josephus not as Yoseph bar Matthiyah — as he was known during the war against Rome — but as Josephus (and usually Flavius Josephus in our libraries, taking the designation from the Flavian emperors who were his protectors). His program throughout his work is to serve as an apologist of Judaism within a Hellenistic environment. He argues in his *Jewish War,* written shortly after the unsuccessful revolt, that the leadership in Jerusalem and its priesthood (including himself) were only involved in the war because of the pressure of extremists. Good priests such as Ananus the high priest were heroes of moderation (*War* 4 §§319–25), and Josephus envisions the Temple as functioning once again under the aegis of the Roman empire (*War* 5

§19). Of course, that argument is quite a case to make from a former general of the Jews in Galilee! But Josephus claims within the work that a revelation convinced him that all power had passed to the Romans (see *War* 3 §§351–54; 6 §§312–13). They were to rule, but his priestly pedigree, his prophetic insight, and his practical experience in government made Josephus, in his recommendation of himself to his Roman overlords, the ideal master of a restored Temple.[6]

Between Josephus's *Jewish War* and his *Antiquities* there is another twenty years[7] and another, smaller (but — here again — convenient) conversion. Ananus the hero of the *War* is now the thug who illegally killed James (Yakob), the brother of Yeshua (*Antiquities* 20 §§197–203). How is it that, twenty years after writing the *War*, Josephus now conveniently remembers things about Yeshua, Yohanan, and Yakob which he had not mentioned before? On the one hand, the persecution of Christians in Rome was by the time he came to write his *Antiquities* quite out of fashion. Even Tacitus, his near contemporary, criticizes Nero's excesses in that regard.[8] What Tacitus says about Nero and the Christians may

---

6. See "Joseph bar Matthias's Vision of the Temple," Bruce Chilton, *The Temple of Jesus: His Sacrificial Program within a Cultural History of Sacrifice* (University Park: Pennsylvania State University Press, 1992), 69–87.

7. See Mason, *Josephus and the New Testament*, 53–84 for a chronology of Josephus's writings.

8. See *Annals* 15.37–44 in Bruce Chilton and Jacob Neusner, *Trading Places: Sourcebook* (Cleveland: Pilgrim, 1997), 182–87.

be compared to what Josephus says about Ananus in the case of Yakob, about Herod Antipas in the case of Yohanan, and about Pilate in the case of Yeshua. Christianity was a long way from being acceptable at the time Josephus wrote the *Antiquities,* but the deadly persecution of Christians was understood to be counterproductive. To this extent, Josephus is writing as the good Roman he became when he realized all power had passed to the Romans. But this consideration also explains why Josephus mentions heroes of Christianity in what seems to be a sympathetic way. Why does he also, and in direct opposition to his earlier characterization, denigrate Ananus?

Just as the position of Christians within Judaism (and moving outside Judaism) had shifted in the twenty years between Josephus's *War* and his *Antiquities,* so the positions of priests and Pharisees had changed, almost to the point of being exchanged. So now the priests who had once been praised are portrayed as bringing about Jerusalem's destruction, and the Pharisees who were once blamed for giving a reverent and rather simple Queen Alexandra bad advice (*War* 1 §111) are portrayed as enjoying mass support (*Antiquities* 13 §298), and Alexandra is depicted as mad for power (*Antiquities* 13 §417). Because Josephus's story is long and complicated (and his ethics even more so), there is no question of any complete change or fabrication on his part. Nonetheless, by the end of his life (in his *Life*), Josephus describes himself as having been a Pharisee all along (*Life* §12). Rather surprising when we consider it was Pharisees that

Josephus blamed for trying to get him removed as general from Galilee during the time of the revolt (see *Life* §197). But that, he hastens to explain, was the consequence of envy, bribery, and high priestly connivance, and in any case pious Josephus defeated them all, blessed by another vision (see *Life* §§189–270).

The point of our discussion of Josephus is not just a general warning about his reliability. Being aware of his interests in no way diminishes his significance; it only enables us to use his testimony, the only extant history by a contemporary of Jesus which survived the period, with appropriate care. Correcting for his interests, we gain an insight into the events and movements of his time.

When he describes himself as a Pharisee from the age of nineteen, Josephus directly compares the Pharisees to the Stoics (*Life* §12), whose teaching was then emerging as the most popular philosophy in the Roman empire. He would certainly have been aware of the career of Seneca, a famed Stoic, tutor of the emperor Nero and statesman, who died by his own hand rather than succumb to Nero's violence.[9] In a letter to his friend Lucilius, Seneca praises philosophy as that which "forms and builds the soul, orders life, rules conduct, manifests what is to be done and not done, sits at the helm and directs the course through the dangers of waves" (Letter 16 §3). That definition, of course, raises the question

---

9. For a very brief introduction and the text here cited, see Richard M. Gummere, *Seneca in Ten Volumes,* vol. 4: *Ad Lucilium Epistulae Morales,* Loeb Classical Library 75 (Cambridge: Harvard University Press, 1989).

whether the power of philosophy might even overcome fate, and to that Seneca gives a qualified answer, affirming no simple response to the question of whether human life is predetermined (Letter 16 §§4–6).

That qualified response is of particular interest, because Josephus says of the Pharisees that they side completely with neither fate nor free will as the explanation of human destiny (so *War* 2 §§162–63 and *Antiquities* 18 §13): events may be attributed to fate, but that does not remove the duty of the soul to behave rightly. That agrees so closely with what Seneca says, it seems clear that Josephus is deliberately portraying the Pharisees in terms of Stoicism.[10] Since the Pharisees' own interest centered on issues of purity,[11] the extent of Josephus's special pleading seems obvious. That apologetic factor needs to be taken into account in assessing what Josephus has to say about Yohanan the immerser.[12]

Yohanan is not the only immerser whom Josephus portrays. He says after his reference to his study with the Essenes,

---

10. In this regard, see Shaye J. D. Cohen, *Josephus in Galilee and Rome: His Vita and Development as a Historian,* Columbia Studies in the Classical Tradition 8 (Leiden: Brill, 1979).

11. See Jacob Neusner, *The Pharisees: Rabbinic Perspectives,* Studies in Ancient Judaism 1 (Hoboken, N.J.: Ktav, 1973); "Josephus' Pharisees: A Complete Repertoire," in *Josephus, Judaism, and Christianity,* ed. L. H. Feldman and G. Hata (Detroit: Wayne State University Press, 1987), 274–92.

12. This point is made generally by Mason, *Josephus and the New Testament,* 154.

> Thinking it insufficient experience for myself from
> that quarter, I heard of a certain person named
> Bannus who stayed in the wilderness, wearing
> clothing from trees, supported by food which grows
> of itself, washing with cold water day and night
> and frequently for sanctification, and I became his
> zealot. (*Life* §11)

The correspondence to Yohanan is striking, in that the
washing is for sanctification, and he takes disciples. Indeed, we might observe further that, when Josephus
describes himself as Bannus's "zealot," that is comparable
to the characterization of a certain Simon as a "zealot" in
the list of Yeshua's disciples (see Luke 6:15). Zeal is something one might bring to a relationship with a teacher,
quite aside from the question of a political agenda.

But it is Josephus's own language which raises the possibility of a political dimension of discipleship (and not
just in respect to Jesus' disciples). After all, it is Josephus
who calls the hard-line revolutionaries who seized control of the Temple during the revolt of 66–70 by the
name they took, that of "zealots" (see *War* 4 §§158–
397). The only problem has been that scholarship has
tended to treat that group as if it were a definite party
within Judaism long before the revolt, but there is no
denying that a "zealot" at any time might become aggres-
sive to the point of violence in his dedication. Josephus
himself, by his own testimony (as we have seen), joined
forces with the revolt after his study of Pharisaism and
his period as Bannus's zealot.

We need to hold open the possibility, therefore, that Yohanan (and Bannus for that matter) were not only considered to be politically threatening, but could become programmatically threatening to the established order. Yet remaining open to that suggestion is not the same as proving it. There has been a tendency to class Yohanan with the people whom Josephus calls "false prophets," whose followers presumably called them prophets. In fact, Josephus simply calls Yohanan a good man and describes his commitment and Bannus's commitment to sanctification by bathing in approving terms. Nothing they did (as related by Josephus) can be compared with what Josephus said the false prophets did: one scaled Mount Gerezim to find the vessels deposited by Moses (*Antiquities* 18 §§85–87); Theudas waited at the Jordan for the waters to part for him, as they had for Joshua (*Antiquities* 20 §§97–98)[13]; the Egyptian marched from the Mount of Olives in the hope the walls of Jerusalem might fall at his command (*Antiquities* 20 §§169–72) so that he might conquer Jerusalem (*War* 2 §§261–63). If there is an act in the Gospels which approximates to such fanaticism, it is Yeshua's

---

13. According to Colin Brown, Theudas was inspired by Yohanan, whose program was not purification but a recrossing of the Jordan; see "What Was John the Baptist Doing?" *Bulletin for Biblical Research* 7 (1997): 48. That seems a desperate expedient to avoid Yohanan's obvious connection with purification. The equally obvious obstacles are that crossing the Jordan is not a part of any characterization of Yohanan's message in the primary sources, and that Josephus does not associate Yohanan with the "false prophets."

entry into Jerusalem and his occupation of the Temple; apparently he expected to prevail against all the odds in insisting upon his own understanding of what true purity there was, in opposition to Caiaphas and the imposing authority of a high priest sanctioned by Rome. When Yeshua is styled a prophet in Matthew 21:11, 46, that may have something to do with the usage of Josephus, but to portray Yohanan in such terms is incautious.

This brings us to one of the principal difficulties in evaluating Yohanan. Because he is foundational within the preaching of the Gospels, he serves as a foil to whatever image of Yeshua is preferred. Yohanan is law, Yeshua is grace; Yohanan is about judgment, Yeshua is about salvation; the one plays the Old Testament to the other's New Testament,[14] and so forth. And Yohanan is a prophet in the mold of Josephus's fanatics, while Yeshua is a wise teller of timeless parables. The problem is, of course, that "prophet" is just the designation Josephus withholds from Yohanan, and Yohanan is identified as a prophet only as a consequence of Yeshua's observation that Yohanan is "a prophet, and more than a prophet" (so Matt. 11:9/Luke 7:26).

---

14. The duality is especially obvious in the paradigm of Sanders, in which John the Baptist upholds "covenantal nomism" and Jesus denies the necessity for repentance. See Bruce Chilton, "Jesus and the Repentance of E. P. Sanders," *Tyndale Bulletin* 39 (1988): 1–18.

Yohanan's Program within the Practice of Purity

The significance of Yeshua's remark will concern us in a later section (see below pp. 56–57). The point at the moment is that Yohanan is known as a prophet only as a consequence of the estimate of him in the Gospels (see Matt. 14:5; Matt. 21:26/Mark 11:32/Luke 20:6. In the case of the last three passages, it is telling that what is a narrative comment in Mark is attributed by direct discourse to the Judaic authorities in Matthew and Luke. Yohanan's repute as a prophet is, as far as the evidence attests, a Christian evaluation which would at the earliest derive from Yeshua himself.

In order to evaluate Yohanan within his own terms of reference, we need to return to Josephus's characterization. Both Yohanan and Bannus are presented as figures focused on the issue of "sanctification" (*hagnaia*) by means of washing. But there are three related features which distinguish Yohanan from Bannus within Josephus's presentation. First, a large following is attributed to Yohanan, while Bannus is a relatively solitary figure (except for apparently occasional disciples such as Josephus). Second, there is a deliberately public dimension involved in Yohanan's preaching, which leads to his execution at the hands of Herod Antipas. Third, Yohanan does not make ablution a simply personal practice, but urges the activity upon those who come to him. In a word, Yohanan makes immersion a public program, which both earns him his nickname and distinguishes him from Bannus.

The practice of frequent ablutions at Qumran has led to a comparison of Yohanan with the Essenes. That comparison has been somewhat complicated by the issue of whether the covenanters of Qumran and the Essenes are identifiable. A collation of Josephus, Philo, Pliny, and the scrolls nonetheless results in a reasonably coherent picture, which has been masterfully represented by Todd H. Beall.[15] Although the precise identity of those who described themselves as entering what they took to be the true community of Israel will no doubt continue to be debated, the association with the wider movement of the Essenes must be regarded as well established.

Robert H. Eisenman, on the other hand, stresses that Pliny was writing in the period after the revolt in *Natural History* 5.15 when he described the Essenes as living on the western shore of the Dead Sea with Engedi below them.[16] His contention is that the community of the scrolls centered on James the brother of Yeshua, whom he identifies as the righteous teacher. But his own reading of Pliny must also confront an anachro-

---

15. See Todd H. Beall, *Josephus's Description of the Essenes Illustrated by the Dead Sea Scrolls,* Society of New Testament Studies Monograph Series 58 (Cambridge: Cambridge University Press, 1988), a citation and comprehensive discussion of both the texts and the issues.

16. The passage is wrongly cited as 5.17 by Eisenman; see *James the Just in the Habakkuk Pesher,* Studia Post-Biblica 35 (Leiden: Brill, 1986), 83, 84. For a popularized version of his theories, see Eisenman, *James the Brother of Jesus: The Key to Unlocking the Secrets of Early Christianity and the Dead Sea Scrolls* (New York: Viking, 1996).

nism: Qumran was destroyed by the Romans in 68 C.E.[17] Whomever Pliny described was living in conditions ill suited for habitation, or at some site other than Qumran, or in fact dwelled there at an earlier period. In that Pliny appears to be referring to a site which had not been destroyed and Qumran suits the location as described, the most plausible explanation is that he is describing an earlier setting on the basis of his authorities (a list of which he provides in book 1). And the earlier setting, of course, would not allow time for a sect to have emerged which venerated the dead James. In addition, Eisenman's theory must impute to James specifically Essene views, which there is no record that he held, and does not explain why the memory of James was venerated the way it was within the church. Finally, he must also suppose that the deposit of the scrolls in the caves nearby had nothing whatever to do with the history of earlier habitation at Qumran. It is not at all clear that the theory explains anything sufficiently important to compensate for the obscurity it generates.[18]

The Essene movement appears to have its origins

---

17. For a discussion of the archaeology of Qumran, see Roland de Vaux, *Archaeology and the Dead Sea Scrolls* (London: Oxford University Press, 1973), 1–45.

18. Similar theories hold that the righteous teacher was Jesus (J. L. Teicher, "Puzzling Passages in the Damascus Fragments," *Journal of Jewish Studies* 5 [1954]: 139–43) and John the Baptist (B. E. Thiering, *The Gospels and Qumran: A New Hypothesis*, Australian and New Zealand Studies in Theology and Religion [Sydney: Theological Explorations, 1981]). Mutatis mutandis, the same objections apply to them.

in opposition to the Hasmoneans. They pursued their own system of purity, ethics, and initiation, followed their own calendar, and withdrew into their own communities, either within cities or in isolated sites such as Qumran.[19] There they awaited a coming apocalyptic war, when they, as "the sons of light," would triumph over "the sons of darkness": not only the Gentiles, but anyone not of their vision (see *The Manual of Discipline* and *The War of the Sons of Light and the Sons of Darkness*). The culmination of those efforts was to involve complete control of Jerusalem and the Temple, where worship would be offered according to their revelation, the correct understanding of the law of Moses (see *Zadokite Document* 5:17–6:11). Their insistence upon a doctrine of two messiahs, one of Israel and one of Aaron, would suggest that it was particularly the Hasmoneans' arrogation of priestly and royal powers which alienated the Essenes, and such a usurpation of what the Essenes considered divine prerogatives also characterized Herodian settlements with Rome.

On a routine level the Essenes appear to have focused on the issue of purity, thus maintaining a tense relationship with the cultic establishment which comported well with their apocalyptic expectation that control of the Temple would one day be theirs. Some of them lived in cities, where they performed ablutions, maintained dis-

---

19. See David Flusser, "The Social Message from Qumran," *Judaism and the Origins of Christianity* (Jerusalem: Magnes, 1988), 193–201.

tinctive dietary regulations, observed stricter controls on marital relations than was common, and regulated the offerings they brought to the Temple according to their own constructions of purity. A more extreme form of the movement lived apart from cities in communities such as Qumran: in them celibacy and a break with ordinary sacrificial worship were the rule. The aim throughout, however, was the eventual governance of the Temple by Essene priests, the first phase of the war of the sons of light against the sons of darkness.

The practice of regular ablutions at Qumran shows that Bannus, Yohanan the immerser, and the Pharisees were in no sense unique, or even unusual, in their insistence upon such practices. But the entire direction of Essene practice, the interest in the actual control of worship in the Temple, appears unlike Yohanan's. The notion that Yohanan somehow opposed the cult in the Temple is weakly based. The argument is sometimes mounted that, because Yohanan preached a baptism of repentance for the forgiveness of sins, he challenged the efficacy of sacrificial forgiveness.[20] Such assertions invoke a supposed dualism between moral and cultic

---

20. See Webb, *John the Baptist and Prophet,* 192, 193. Webb's claims are ultimately based upon Joseph Thomas, *Le mouvement baptiste en Palestine et Syrie (150 av. J.C.–300 ap. J.C.)* (Gembloux: Duculot, 1935). But the thesis of a widespread movement of "nonconformity" in which there was a substitution of "baptizing rites for the observation of Temple sacrifice" was long ago discredited by Matthew Black, "Patristic Accounts of Jewish Sects," *The Scrolls and Christian Origins* (London: Nelson, 1961), 54.

atonement which simply has no place in the critical discussion of early Judaism,[21] and they in no way suffice
to establish that Yohanan opposed worship in the Temple. The motif of his preaching "a baptism of repentance
for the forgiveness of sins" may in any case represent
the anachronistic assignment to Yohanan of an element
of the language of catechesis within early Christianity.
The phrase appears in Mark 1:4 and Luke 3:3 (see 1:77)
in relation to Yohanan, but a variant appears in obviously Christian contexts in Matthew 26:28 and Luke
24:47. Webb can see the problem posed for his thesis
by such passages as Acts 2:38, and his only defense is a
methodological bias against any "skeptical conclusion."[22]
Josephus more accurately observed that Yohanan's baptism was not understood to seek pardon for sins, but to
purify the body (*Antiquities* 18 §117).

The motif of Yohanan's priesthood (adduced by Webb
on p. 193) is similarly beside the point of any alleged
antagonism to worship in the Temple. The fact of being
born a priest did not necessarily involve anyone in the
Temple on a regular basis, although it might conceivably
have prompted the increased concern with purity which

---

21. Even within the sacrificial systems of the Hebrew Bible, the
link between purity and righteousness is implicit, and the Psalms
bring to open expression the systemic association of righteousness
and purity (see 18:21 [v. 20 in English versions]; 24:3–6; 26:4–7;
51:4, 8, 9, 12 [English vv. 2, 6, 7, 10]; 119:9). See Chilton, *The Temple of Jesus*, chap. 4, "Sacrifice in 'Classic' Israel," 45–67, and chap. 7,
"The Sacrificial Program of Jesus," 113–36.

22. Webb, *John the Baptist and Prophet*, 171.

evidently characterized Yohanan. Even so, the fact that he was a priest did not imbue Josephus with a marked sensitivity to the issue. He had no scruples regarding where Jews in Syria were to buy their oil (see *The Jewish War* 2 §§590–94) and expressed none in regard to fighting on the Sabbath or dealing with the uncleanness occasioned by corpses.[23] He mentions Herod's construction of the golden eagle in the Temple only when certain (apparently Pharisaic) rabbis object to it, and ventures no vigorous opinion of his own (1 §648–50). The only time he refers to the impurity of food, an issue which must have plagued many military campaigns during the period, is in order to assail the impiety of Yohanan of Gischala at the end of the war (7 §264).[24]

Some priests, especially among the privileged families in Jerusalem, were notoriously pro-Roman. The story of sons of the high priest having the surgery called *"epispasm"* in order to restore the appearance of a foreskin (for gymnastic purposes) is well known (see 1 Macc. 1:14, 15; *Antiquities* 12 §240, 241). There is little doubt that such families, the most prominent of which were the Sadducees and Boethusians, were not highly re-

---

23. See his attention to the lapse at a later period in *Antiquities* 3 §262.

24. Reference might be made in this regard to Josephus's fascination with menstrual blood for such diverse purposes as removing asphalt (4 §480) and neutralizing the supposed movements of the Baaras root (7 §181), which he expresses without compunction, although he knows quite well that menstruants are to be excluded from the Temple (5 §227).

garded by most Jews (see b. Pesahim 57a). They are typically portrayed in a negative light, as not teaching the resurrection of the dead (see *War* 2 §165; Matt. 22:23; Mark 12:18; Luke 20:27; Acts 23:8), but the issue may have been one of emphasis: the Torah had stressed that correct worship in the Temple would bring with it material prosperity, and the elite priests attempted to realize that promise. The arrangement gave them such consistent control that they became known as "high priests," although there was in fact only one high priest. But Josephus, as well as the Gospels, indulges in the usage, so that it should not be taken as an inaccuracy: the plural is a cultic mistake, but a sociological fact.

Members of most priestly families were not "high priests"[25] and did not in any sense exercise control over the Temple, or even participate ordinarily in the conduct of worship there. The well-known rotas of 1 Chronicles 23; 24; Ezra 2:36–39; 10:18–22; Nehemiah 10:2–9; 12:1–7, 12–21; *Antiquities* 7 §§365, 366; *Life* §2; *Against Apion* 2 §108 provided for only occasional service (see Luke 1:8, 9). Within the Gospels, priests appear locally, in adjudications of purity (Matt. 8:1–4; Mark 1:40–45; Luke 5:12–16; see Luke 10:31; 17:14, and the exceptional role of Zechariah in 1:5–23), while high priests

---

25. For a brief discussion of the passages, see Joseph A. Fitzmyer, *The Gospel According to Luke (I–IX),* Anchor Bible (Garden City, N.Y.: Doubleday, 1981), 322; the standard remains Joachim Jeremias, *Jerusalem in the Time of Jesus,* trans. F. H. and C. H. Cave (London: SCM, 1969), 98–207.

are essentially limited to Jerusalem or use Jerusalem as a base of power (see Matt. 2:4; 16:21; 20:18; 21:15, 23, 45; 26:1–28:11; Mark 8:31; 10:33; 11:18, 27; 14:1–15:31; Luke 3:2; 9:22; 19:47; 20:1–24:20; John 1:19; 7:32, 45; 11:47, 49, 51, 57; 12:10; 18:3–19:21). Several priests were also prominent in the revolt against Rome, however, and it should not be thought that such priestly nationalists, among whom were Yoseph bar Matthiyah, better known as Flavius Josephus, emerged only at the end of the sixties (*War* 2 §§562–68). The precedent of the Hasmoneans was there for any priestly family to see as a possible alternative to Roman rule, direct or indirect. Indeed, some priests were not only nationalists, but revolutionaries, who joined with the Essenes, or with rebellious Pharisees, although any alliance with a prophetic pretender is, perhaps, not a likely supposition. In any case, Yohanan well may not have been a priest: the claim that he was is weakly attested (Luke 1:5), and made within the same complex of material which asserts that Jesus was related to him (see Luke 1:36), although of Davidic ancestry (see 1:27 and 1:69). The line which divides historical reminiscence from theological typology is particularly difficult to draw here.

Once it is appreciated that Yohanan is not known to have shared the cultic program of the Essenes, the argument that he is to be associated with the covenanters of Qumran loses its foundation. W. H. Brownlee gave currency to the view that the usage of Isaiah 40 in *The Manual of Discipline* viii.14; ix.19 shows that "John must have been familiar with Essene thoughts regarding the coming of the Messianic age."[26] More accurately, one might say that the analogy suggests that Isaiah 40 was known both to the covenanters and to the Christians who revered Yohanan's memory as their master's forerunner. To build upon such analogies and Luke 1:80 the speculation that John was orphaned and raised by the Essenes is an exercise in hagiography.

Essene practice, together with that of the Pharisees, Sadducees, and Bannus, does nonetheless suggest by analogy a likely feature of Yohanan's baptism which contemporary discussion has obscured. It is routinely claimed that Yohanan preached a "conversionary repentance" by baptism, an act once for all which was not repeatable nor to be repeated.[27] That is a fine description of baptism as portrayed in the Epistle to the Hebrews 6:1–8, and such a theology of baptism once and for all came to predominate within catholic Christianity (for reasons we will see in chapter 4). But ablutions in Judaism were characteristically repeatable, and therefore Hebrews must argue against the proposition that one might be baptized afresh. Hebrews marks the conscious

---

26. W. H. Brownlee, "John the Baptist in the New Light of Ancient Scrolls," *Interpretation* 9 (1955): 73; see Jean Steinmann, *John the Baptist and the Desert Tradition* (New York: Harper, 1958), 59.

27. See Webb, *John the Baptist and Prophet,* 197–202. Brownlee, "John the Baptist in the New Light of Ancient Scrolls," 76, realized at an early stage that Essene ablutions could not be regarded as an initiation.

realization that Judaic immersion and Christian baptism have parted company. Only the attribution to Yohanan of a later, catholic theology of baptism can justify the characterization of his baptism as symbol of a definitive "conversion."

Part of the reason for which the later Christian theology of baptism has been telescoped into the first century is that the sources of Rabbinic Judaism have been (mis)interpreted as attesting the institution of "proselyte baptism" as a rite in its own terms.[28] There is no doubt that one was immersed as part of accepting the way of life laid down in the Torah, but there is no indication whatever that the first immersion in the case of a proselyte (convert) was in principle any different from the frequent immersions which would normally eventuate in the practice of any Israelite. On the contrary, the discussions in Mishnah treat of the immersion of a proselyte under the same category as ordinary immersion (see Pesahim 8:8; Eduyyoth 5:2): after all, the foreskin from which a male convert separated himself was unclean. In fact, the understanding of Rabbinica underscores how Christian practice during the first century emerged as distinct from the usual understanding of Judaism and at the same time confirms that the ordinary assumption

---

28. Above all, see Albrecht Oepke's article in *Theological Dictionary of the New Testament*, trans. G. W. Bromiley (Grand Rapids: Eerdmans, 1964), 1:529–46. The tradition goes on in Lars Hartman, *"Into the Name of the Lord Jesus": Baptism in the Early Church*, Studies of the New Testament and Its World (Edinburgh: Clark, 1997), 5–6.

within Judaism was that ablutions were repeatable and repeated.[29]

If Yohanan's baptism was not in the interests of "conversion," or permanent purification, or opposition to atonement by means of cultic sacrifice, what was its purpose? Josephus in *Antiquities* 18 §117 asserts that Yohanan's immersion was to serve as a ritual of purity following a return to righteousness. Righteousness and bathing together made one pure. Josephus makes a nearly or actually dualistic distinction between the righteousness which effects purification of the soul and the baptism which symbolizes the consequent purification of the body, and that is consistent with his portrayal of others with whom he expresses sympathy, the Essenes, the Pharisees, and Bannus.[30]

Webb argues that Yohanan attempted to found a sect after the manner of the Essenes.[31] The thesis founders

---

29. In a recent article, Colin Brown has claimed that "John's activity looks increasingly like a different kind of purification altogether"; see "What Was John the Baptist Doing?" *Bulletin for Biblical Research* 7 (1997): 43 n. 21. But that conviction is buttressed only by secondary literature, which reflects that view among Christians that Yohanan (like Yeshua) must have been unlike contemporary Judaism.

30. See Webb, *John the Baptist and Prophet*, 192, and Chilton, *The Temple of Jesus*, chap. 5, "Joseph bar Matthias's Vision of the Temple," 69–87. In her otherwise excellent study, Joan E. Taylor accords Josephus too much objectivity and therefore attributes such dualism to Yohanan, as well as an almost Rabbinic devotion to the Torah; see *The Immerser: John the Baptist within Second Temple Judaism*, Studying the Historical Jesus 2 (Grand Rapids: Eerdmans, 1997), 261–64.

31. See Webb, *John the Baptist and Prophet*, 197–202. His stance is

on several considerations. There is no evidence whatever that baptism for Yohanan constituted an initiation, comparable to the ceremony for novices at Qumran.[32] It is not even to be assumed — as we have seen — that baptism for Yohanan was not to be repeated. Moreover, no discipline but "righteousness" was required by Yohanan, as far as the available evidence would suggest. His execution was not occasioned by placing an unusual requirement upon Antipas, but for insisting Antipas keep the Torah of purity as any person might understand it, by not taking his brother's wife (see Lev. 20:21).

The purpose of Yohanan's baptism must be sought, not in an unfounded hypothesis of sectarian motivations, but in the nature of his activity as compared to ordinary practices of purification. It is here that contemporary students of Yohanan have been most misled by the supposition that he was a prophet with a recoverable message which explains his activity. Historically, his activity is itself as much of his program as we are ever likely to grasp. Yohanan practiced his immersion in natural sources of water. It is sometimes taken that his purpose was to use living water (see Webb, p. 195), but that is not specified in any source, and the waters of the Jordan or a pool in Peraea or an oasis in the valley of

---

that of Steinmann, *John the Baptist,* 5, and opposed to that of Wink, *John the Baptist in the Gospel Tradition,* 107. He discusses neither.

32. Indeed, David Flusser contrasts John's stance with the Essenes on the precise issue of initiation; see "The Social Message from Qumran," 109.

the Jordan would not necessarily be flowing.[33] Indeed, Sanders has plausibly suggested that water from a spring was equated with the category of naturally collected water by the first century.[34] Moreover, even if Yohanan did use living water by preference, the especial corruption of what was to be purified was not thereby marked, as is sometimes supposed (see Webb, 193): corpse contamination, after all, was dealt with by means of the still water of the ashes of the red heifer, not living water (see Num. 19).[35] Yohanan's baptism made no statement as to the nature of what was to be purified: his activity took that as being as self-evident as Antipas's lapse. Yohanan's baptism was, however, an implicit claim that there was no advantage in the pools of Qumran, the double-vatted miqvaoth of the Pharisees, or the private baths of aristocratic groups such as the Sadducees.[36] In contrast, for example, to the insistence that no less than forty seahs were required for pure water and that a second vat of forty seahs could be used to purify a vat whose cleanness had become subject to doubt (in the Mishnah, see Miq-

---

33. See Herbert G. May, with G. N. S. Hunt, R. W. Hamilton, and J. Day, *Oxford Bible Atlas* (New York: Oxford University Press, 1984), 50.

34. See E. P. Sanders, *Jewish Law from Jesus to the Mishnah* (Philadelphia: Trinity Press International, 1990), 215.

35. For an indication of how the ashes and the water were regarded by Pharisees and rabbis, see Parah 5:1–8.11.

36. See Sanders, *Jewish Law,* 214–27, for a preliminary discussion. The later development of the immersion of proselytes (see Yebamoth 47a, b) accords with the understanding that such bathing is an ordinary act of integration within Israel.

vaot 6:8; 7:6), Yohanan reverted to the provision of living water in the wilderness. He enacted what amounted to generic purification, in contrast to the deliberate artifice involved in several other movements, sectarian and non-sectarian. In that sense, his purpose was deliberately anti-sectarian.

For those living in Judaea, Peraea, Galilee, and even Samaria (see John 3:23), Yohanan's immersion would have had a great appeal. Miqvaoth may not have been available to them, and — even when available — they may not have met with approval from those with specialist teachings about bathing such as the Pharisees and Essenes.[37] What Yohanan offered in the wilderness, at or near the river which marked the territorial promise of Israel, was a generic immersion, which could meet real and potential objections to the purity of those who were immersed after the pattern Yohanan set. The appeal might have been especially great for those who were on the way to the Temple. Although the Temple itself was endowed with a system for ritual ablution,[38] even to get to the point of being able to immerse oneself in the vicinity

---

37. See Lee I. Levine, "The Second Temple Synagogue: The Formative Years," *The Synagogue in Late Antiquity,* A Publication of the Jewish Theological Seminary in America (Philadelphia: American Schools of Oriental Research, 1987), 7–31; Hanan Eshal, "A Note on 'Miqvaot' at Sepphoris," *Archaeology and the Galilee: Texts and Contexts in the Graeco-Roman and Byzantine Periods,* South Florida Studies in the History of Judaism 143, ed. D. R. Edwards and C. T. McCollough (Atlanta: Scholars Press, 1997), 131–33.

38. See Chilton, *The Temple of Jesus,* 91–111.

of the Temple required that one be accepted within the company of worshipers. And Mishnah (Hagigah 2:7) attests that for some the clothing of ordinary people was to be regarded as in a state of uncleanness such as would be produced from contact with genital discharge.

Inferentially, it might be maintained that Yohanan's baptism was driven by an eschatological expectation, not necessarily of a messiah, but of divine judgment.[39] Of all the statements attributed to Yohanan, the claim that after him a baptism of spirit was to come stands out as possibly authentic.[40] Whether or not it is, the anticipation of imminent judgment would both supply a suitable motivation for Yohanan's activity and help to account for his appropriation within early Christianity. But whatever his own motivation, and those of subsequent interpreters, that he acted as a purifier on the basis of ritual bathing is the most certain — as well as the most obvious — feature of his public activity.

39. See Flusser, "The Magnificat, the Benedictus and the War Scroll," *Judaism*, 148.

40. See Webb, *John the Baptist and Prophet*, 262–78. His citation of Jubilees 1:23 on p. 224 is especially apposite. The phrase "and fire" in the version of Mark 1:8 reflected in Matthew 3:11/Luke 3:16 is, however, probably an apologetic addition inspired by Malachi 3:2.

≈ 2 ≈

The Political Crisis of Yohanan and Yeshua

Herod Antipas's Execution of Yohanan the Immerser

Josephus refers to Yohanan in what must seem to be an unusual context. Considerably after Yohanan's death, he speaks of a war between Herod Antipas and Aretas IV, the king of Nabataea. In 36 C.E., Aretas's forces were ordered into battle quite suddenly in the course of a border dispute, with the result that "all the army of Herod was destroyed" according to Josephus (*Antiquities* 18 §114). Even allowing for the exaggeration for which Josephus is justly famous, it is evident that he is referring to major armed conflict between two of Rome's client rulers. Their kingdoms may be described as petty in comparison with the empire, but they occupied the vital buffer zone in the Near East between Rome and the Parthian empire, which during this period was a serious and militarily powerful rival.

The Roman emperor Tiberius ordered Vitellius, the

Roman legate to Syria who had overall charge of both petty kingdoms, to bring Aretas back in chains if captured alive or to send his head back to Rome if he died during the battle that seemed inevitable (*Antiquities* 18 §115). Vitellius was actually embarked on this punitive expedition, in the course of which he attended festal sacrifice in the Temple in Jerusalem with Herod Antipas, when news reached him of Tiberius's death and Gaius's accession. That ended Vitellius's authority to make war and signaled a profound change in Roman policy in the Near East (*Antiquities* 18 §§120–256).[1]

Still, Aretas's campaign seemed completely unwarranted to the Romans, and Vitellius's expedition against him was welcomed by Jews in Jerusalem (*Antiquities* 18 §123). But Josephus reports that some Jews thought that the annihilation of Herod Antipas's army came justly from divine providence because of what he had done to Yohanan. That is when Yohanan's activity is described. Surprisingly, however, only a general motivation is supplied for Herod's imprisonment of Yohanan at Machaerus and the subsequent execution: as crowds began to be added to the usual throng around Yohanan, Herod feared that an insurrection (*stasis*) might result and decided to act quickly against the possibility (*Antiquities* 18 §§116–19).

When it comes to the reasons for the enmity between Herod and Aretas, however, Josephus is quite specific. Herod Antipas decided to marry Herodias, who was

---

1. See David F. Graf, "Aretas," *Anchor Bible Dictionary*, ed. D. N. Freedman (New York: Doubleday, 1992), 1:373–76.

at the time married to his brother.[2] Antipas was also married — to Aretas's daughter! She got wind of her approaching divorce. But before Antipas could act, she received permission from him to go to Machaerus, a fortress to the east of the Dead Sea, and (having sent messengers in advance) made a journey from Machaerus back to her father. So began Aretas's hatred of his one-time son-in-law (see *Antiquities* 18 §§109–13).

Now it is at this same Machaerus that Antipas has Yohanan killed, and it seems evident from Josephus that there is some connection between Yohanan and the soap opera which led to the war. The Gospels in this case provide us with more specifics (Mark 6:14–29 and Matt. 14:1–12), and they enable us to make sense of what Josephus says. They tell us the well-known story of Yohanan's imprisonment and of a birthday celebration for Herod Antipas. Herodias, Antipas's new wife and mother of Salome (certainly the most legendary dancer ever!), has her daughter ask for Yohanan's head when the king asks her to name her gift for pleasing him and his guests so thoroughly. She does just that.

That may seem to be a far cry from Josephus's report

---

2. Josephus names this brother as "Herod" and describes him as a half-brother (*Antiquities* 18 §109). He is named as Philip in the Gospels (see Matt. 14:3; Mark 6:17; some manuscripts of Luke 3:19), but that seems to be a confusion with Herodias's son-in-law; so Louis H. Feldman, *Josephus* 9, The Loeb Classical Library 433 (Cambridge: Harvard University Press, 1992), 76–77. The correction away from "Philip" in some manuscripts of Luke attests the awareness of the error, and the omission of the name is the preferred reading in Luke.

of the king's general fear of insurrection, but there are in fact important links between Josephus and the Gospels. They report Herod's recognition that Yohanan was "a righteous and holy man" (so Mark 6:20), while for Josephus he was "a good man" dedicated to righteousness and sanctification (*Antiquities* 18 §§116–18). Moreover, the Gospels specify the reason for Herod's fear of Yohanan: Yohanan had specifically insisted that Herod could not marry his brother's wife (Mark 6:18). That insistence follows directly from applying Leviticus 18:16; 20:21: to uncover the nakedness of the brother's wife is to reveal one's own shame and to invite divine punishment. Yohanan was a practitioner and teacher of that purity which was to be accessible to and required of all Israel, Antipas included. His public denunciation of this marriage was a natural extension of his concern, not a isolated and calculated foray into politics.

When we put Josephus and the Gospels together, we can see why Antipas had Yohanan executed at Machaerus. It was not only convenient to the activity of Yohanan in the Jordan Valley, while offering suitable protection from Yohanan's followers; the flight of Aretas's daughter had also made it a place of a symbolic defeat for Antipas, and killing Yohanan enabled Antipas to reclaim it as his domain. But if Mark and Matthew help us to confirm the estimation of Yohanan as a figure concerned with purity and to specify the source of Herod Antipas's deadly hatred of him, their story of Salome's famous dance and its consequence should be used with caution. Although all the elements of the legend cannot be proven to be fictional, in aggregate their purpose is to exculpate Antipas from what only Antipas could be responsible for. There is an obvious analogy with the treatment of Pilate in the Gospels, where he is made to seem the dupe of the system which he was in fact in charge of. In any case, it is notable that Luke's Antipas is more vigorous (see Luke 3:19–20; 9:7–9) and makes his decision quite literally without the song and dance: Salome makes no appearance in Luke. As we proceed, we shall have occasion to appreciate Luke's omissions, additions, and rearrangements.[3]

Recourse to the Gospels also elucidates another feature of what Josephus says. Noting that Yohanan already had a considerable following, he observes that Antipas reacted when he knew the following was increasing yet again. That increase was evidently occasioned by Yohanan's criticism of a marriage which no one observant of the Torah could have approved. Taken together, Josephus and the Gospels clearly outline the political circumstances which brought about the death of Yohanan.

The Consequences of Yohanan's Execution for His Movement and for Yeshua

The material in the Synoptic Gospels which relates the death of Yohanan (Mark 6:14–29 and Matt. 14:1–12)

---

3. For example, Luke alone provides the narrative of Yeshua's appearance before Antipas (Luke 23:6–12).

amounts to an overture to the Passion Narrative of Jesus, complete with an exculpation of Herod Antipas comparable to the exculpation of Pilate (as we have seen). Roman responsibility, even indirectly in Herod's case, is reduced at the cost of increasing Jewish responsibility. It is evident that the apologetic interests of primitive Christian catechesis are served by the passage, but it is equally clear (as we have discovered) that the circumstances of Yohanan's death are reflected here, even as his image is serving to reflect the John the Baptist familiar to Christianity. In its origin, the passage attests to what Josephus tells us directly: Yohanan enjoyed a following, people who took up his practice.

The Gospel according to John reflects that fact quite straightforwardly, although its presentation tails off into a certain amount of confusion. Yohanan's identification of Yeshua as "the lamb of God that removes the sin of the world" causes two of Yohanan's own disciples to follow Yeshua as their rabbi, and they begin to gather other followers (John 1:29–51). The implication is that Yeshua has already been involved in Yohanan's movement. Much of John's Gospel proceeds by implication, because it assumes that its readers are believers who have already been introduced to a catechesis prior to baptism in Jesus' name such as is reflected in the Synoptic Gospels.[4] In

---

4. See Bruce Chilton, *Profiles of a Rabbi: Synoptic Opportunities in Reading about Jesus,* Brown Judaic Studies 177 (Atlanta: Scholars Press, 1989), 139–82, for discussion of John as a post-baptismal, homiletic treatment of the significance of Jesus in relation to the Synoptic Gospels.

the present case, the assumption is that one knows that
Yeshua was baptized by Yohanan, and that during the
course of his association with Yohanan, Yeshua's identity
as God's son became known (see John 1:34 with Matt.
3:17; Mark 1:11; Luke 3:22).

That assumption becomes explicit in what follows
in John's Gospel. Yeshua and his disciples are said to
come into the land of Judaea, where Yeshua remains
with them *and immerses himself* (John 3:22). Although a
later attempt will be made by John to take this assertion
back (John 4:1–3), it is an emphatic and unambiguous
description: Yeshua practiced a ministry of immersion
comparable to Yohanan's. While Yeshua remained in
Judaea, Yohanan himself was immersing his followers
in Aenon near Salem, further north and off the Jordan River, adjacent to the territory of Samaria.[5] Jerome
Murphy-O'Connor suggests that the division of territory
between Yohanan and Yeshua was deliberate: the senior
rabbi took the more difficult task of dealing with Samaritans, while leaving the relatively more straightforward
task of immersing those in Judaea to his disciple.[6]

---

5. See John Rogerson, *Atlas of the Bible* (New York: Facts on File,
1985), 192.

6. See Jerome Murphy-O'Connor, "John the Baptist and Jesus:
History and Hypotheses," *New Testament Studies* 36 (1990): 359–74.
His hypothesis involves identifying Aenon near Salem with Shechem
"in the very heart of Samaritan territory" (365). In an otherwise very
critical treatment of his work, Murphy-O'Connor receives cautious
encouragement for his geographical suggestion from Josef Ernst, "Johannes der Täufer und Jesus von Nazareth in historischer Sicht," *New*

The extension of purity by means of immersion to Samaritans would, of course, have been a notable development. John's Gospel itself observes that Jews do not have dealings with Samaritans (4:9). Yet Yeshua in the story of the Samaritan woman does just that (John 4:4–42),[7] and without offering any particular defense, and he is equally matter of fact in telling the parable of the good Samaritan (Luke 10:30–37). Both the story of the Samaritan woman and the parable of the good Samaritan take it for granted that there is a problem about consorting with Samaritans and that the problem can be overcome. The same perspective is represented in a saying of Yeshua in *The Gospel according to Thomas* (*l.* 60), where he comments on seeing a Samaritan carrying a lamb to Jerusalem(!). If, as Murphy-O'Connor suggests, we take the hint from John 3:23 that Yohanan was already in the process of immersing Samaritans into his generic purification, that would help us to make better sense of Yeshua's attitude toward the Samaritan question. Whatever one might say of his explanation, it seems better than what is offered in John 3:23, that Yohanan

Testament Studies 43 (1997): 167–72. On balance, however, a location closer to the Jordan seems more probable to him (and to me).

7. Jacob's well, which features in the story (John 4:5–6), is actually associated with Shechem in the Old Syriac Gospels, although "Sychar" is the preferred reading. Either way, however, no link with Aenon near Salem is suggested in John, and that is one reason for which Murphy-O'Connor's suggestion is not accepted here. On the location of the well, see Zdravko Stefanovic, "Jacob's Well," *Anchor Bible Dictionary*, ed. D. N. Freedman (New York: Doubleday, 1992), 3:608–9.

was immersing in Aenon near Salem "because there was much water there."

But any picture of easy, harmonious relations between Yohanan and Yeshua is quickly upset in John:

A controversy ensued, therefore, between the disciples of Yohanan with a Jew over purification.

(John 3:25)

Was this unnamed Jew Yeshua? That is an emendation of the text which is frequently suggested, but there is no evidence in manuscripts to support it.[8] But even as the text stands, the disciples of Yohanan enter a controversy concerning purification — which, after all, is the whole point of immersion — and the argument causes them to go on to report Yeshua's activity to Yohanan. They complain about Yeshua's success in immersing, and Yohanan replies with a panegyric which is typical of John's Gospel (John 3:26–36). Unfortunately, they do not speak of what the argument over purification was, nor of where Yohanan and Yeshua stood within it.

To this stage, not enough information has emerged to make it clear how Yohanan and Yeshua might have fallen out over the issue of purification, but the fact of such a disagreement, difficult as it is for the Gospels to attest, seems plain. The political crisis of Yohanan and his follower Yeshua, then, is a crisis in two senses,

---

8. Because the text of the New Testament is so well attested (by more than five thousand Greek manuscripts alone, making for a half million variants), it does not seem prudent to change readings out of purely speculative considerations.

each of which was determinative of the outcome of Yeshua's activity. First, Herod Antipas's execution of Yohanan branded his movement as seditious. Second, purification — the very center of Yohanan's immersion — became a point of contention between that rabbi and his disciple. The consequences of each aspect of the crisis need now to be spelled out.

The Politics of Empire

The Synoptic Gospels are quite plain about when Yeshua's characteristic public ministry began: as Mark 1:14 puts it, "after Yohanan was delivered over" (see the comparable formulations of Matt. 4:12 and Luke 3:19–20[9]). From the point of view of Herod Antipas, Yeshua represented no immediate continuation of Yohanan's threat. That was because in two ways Yeshua stopped doing what Yohanan had been doing.

First and most obviously, Yeshua stopped immersing people as his characteristic activity. Even when we allow — following our previous discussion — that the Gospel according to John reflects Yeshua's acceptance of Yohanan's program of purification, and even if we in-

---

9. One might even conclude from reading Luke's reference in context (prior to Yeshua's immersion) that Yohanan did not personally immerse Yeshua. But that is probably the result of a periodization of their ministries, a treatment of the one and then the other as the key figures in separate epochs (much as Peter and Paul are presented in Acts).

fer that Yeshua might have reverted to that activity from time to time, the simple fact of the matter is that immersion does not become *characteristic* of Yeshua's movement until after the resurrection, and especially in the circle of Peter. Immersion was a prominent part of Yeshua's public program before Yohanan's arrest and death and after Yeshua's resurrection, but not in between, not during the time Yeshua himself directed the course of his movement. Why that was the case remains one of the most obvious — and yet unanswered — questions in the critical study of the New Testament.[10] Why Yeshua stopped immersing is our present concern; why his followers began immersing again after his resurrection will be investigated in the final chapter of our study. For the moment, the point is that no source permits us to infer that Yeshua was known for his immersing after Yohanan's death.

Josephus does not connect Yeshua with Yohanan, although it might have suited his interests to have done so. After all, he is critical of both Pilate and Herod Antipas,[11] so that linking their victims would have been effective in rhetorical terms. Moreover, his theme in discussing Yohanan is the feeling among many Jews that Antipas was justly punished for what he did to Yohanan: to have mentioned the continuation of his activity

---

10. In fact, the question is usually not even posed, so conventional is the assumption that Yohanan was simply there to prepare the way for Yeshua.

11. The similarity of Josephus's criticism of the two is discussed in the last chapter, pp. 7–8.

by Yeshua might have been useful. Obviously, Josephus's silence does not indicate that there was no connection between Yohanan and Yeshua, but the fact that Josephus mentions none does underline what we already know from the Gospels: Yeshua was not known as an immerser, once he entered upon his own characteristic activity.

Nonetheless, there is an implicit connection between Yohanan and Yeshua in the way that Josephus presents them (and the way in which he does not present them). Where Yohanan is described as a "good man" (*Antiquities* 18 §117), Yeshua is called a "wise man," "a doer of miracles," and a rabbi (*Antiquities* 18 §63).[12] Neither of them, it should be stressed, is styled as a prophet by Josephus, because that title (in the form of "false prophet") is reserved for those who lead people against Rome with the symbolic gestures of Moses or Joshua (as we have seen in the last chapter). But in the case of Yohanan, Josephus explains how he became a threat to Herod Antipas. In the case of Yeshua, he simply says that Pilate condemned him to be crucified on the accusation of prominent men (*Antiquities* 18 §64). He reports this after his report of two major controversies concerning the Temple, so we might notice some general similarity to the Synoptic Gospels, but Josephus's theme at this point is Pilate's careless arrogance, not Yeshua's political

---

12. See Zvi Baras, "The *Testimonium Flavianum* and the Martyrdom of James," *Josephus, Judaism, and Christianity*, ed. L. H. Feldman and G. Hata (Detroit: Wayne State University Press, 1987), 338–48.

activity. And whatever the activity which brought about Yeshua's execution, it was not immersion as such, and Josephus does not even attest a connection of Yeshua with Yohanan.

So desisting from immersion put Yeshua in a different category from Yohanan in political terms and afforded Yeshua some protection. The fact of his earlier connection with Yohanan, of course, could scarcely be hidden. Yeshua himself, in opposition to the religious authorities in Jerusalem, would even ask them whether Yohanan's immersion came from God. Such was his teasing response to the question about his own authority (see Mark 11:27–33; Matt. 21:23–27; Luke 20:1–8). By invoking Yohanan's memory, Yeshua reminds his opponents of another teacher who challenged them over the issue of purity and who could rely on considerable popular support. Even before Yeshua again overtly referred to Yohanan, over time, remembrance of the connection to Yohanan would have featured in the opposition to Yeshua. Herod Antipas would hear of Yeshua's miracles and remark, "This is Yohanan raised up" (see Mark 6:14–16; Matt. 14:1–2; Luke 9:7–9). Whatever exactly led Herod Antipas to that conclusion, it was not Yeshua's immersion but his miracles which brought Yeshua to his notice. At the very least, desisting from immersion bought Yeshua time before any confrontation with Herod.[13]

---

13. Luke actually portrays Herod Antipas within the narrative of Yeshua's execution (Luke 23:6–12), and that portrayal is quite plausi-

In addition to desisting from immersion, Yeshua also left the geographical field of Yohanan's activity. He is now no longer in the Jordan Valley, but in Galilee. The Synoptic Gospels are emphatic that Yeshua began to operate there after Yohanan's execution (Mark 1:14; Matt. 4:12; Luke 4:14). It has puzzled commentators for many years that Yeshua would actually be taking up his activity in what one of them called "the lion's den," the center of Herod Antipas's rule.[14] But Josephus has shown us that Peraea, where Yohanan was killed and from which Herod's wife had fled back to Nabataea, was the focus of the dispute which had made Yohanan into a fomenter of sedition. By withdrawing from that region, Yeshua puts space between himself and Herod.

Small villages in Galilee became as characteristic of Yeshua's activity as streams in the Jordan Valley were within Yohanan's.[15] The shift from the wilderness to the village is obviously profound, and we will explore its implications for Yeshua's understanding of purity in

---

ble. See Harold Hoehner, *Herod Antipas* (Grand Rapids: Zondervan, 1980), 224–50.

14. So J. Schmid, *Das Evangelium nach Matthäus* (Regensburg: Pustet, 1959), 70. The matter is discussed in Bruce Chilton, *God in Strength: Jesus' Announcement of the Kingdom,* Studien zum Neuen Testament und seiner Umwelt 1 (Freistadt: Plöchl, 1979), 101–3; reprinted in *The Biblical Seminar* (Sheffield: JSOT, 1987).

15. See James F. Strange, "First-Century Galilee from Archaeology and from the Texts," *Archaeology and the Galilee: Texts and Contexts in the Graeco-Roman and Byzantine Periods,* South Florida Studies in the History of Judaism 143, ed. D. R. Edwards and C. T. McCollough (Atlanta: Scholars Press, 1997), 39–48.

the next section of this chapter. But in political terms, the village provides camouflage for Yeshua. It is not the wilderness and has nothing to do with the Jordan Valley, the place of Yohanan's opposition to Herod Antipas. But it is also quite unlike a city (particularly Sepphoris, a seat of Antipas's power),[16] where Herod's official presence as well as the occupying Romans would be forces to be reckoned with.

Indeed, the danger of Herod Antipas's continuing enmity accounts for what otherwise must seem rather strange. Why does Yeshua, a notably popular rabbi with a diverse following, generally stay away from cities?[17] To some extent, the answer to that question is to be found in Yeshua's program of purity (to be discussed below), but as soon as we make another observation, it becomes clear that another force was also at work. The results when Yeshua actually did enter the one city he did — Jerusalem — were fatal. And Yeshua was conscious of the opponent he was dealing with:

> In that hour some Pharisees came forward, saying to him,

---

16. See the tentative suggestion of Eric M. Meyers, "Jesus and His Galilean Context," in Edwards and McCollough, eds., *Archaeology and the Galilee,* 57–66, 64, within his succinct presentation of Sepphoris on the basis of the literary and archaeological evidence.

17. See Seán Freyne, "The Geography, Politics, and Economics of Galilee and the Quest for the Historical Jesus," *Studying the Historical Jesus: Evaluations of the State of Current Research,* New Testament Tools and Studies 19, ed. B. Chilton and C. A. Evans (Leiden: Brill, 1994), 75–121.

> Get out and go from here! Because Herod
> wants to kill you.

And he said to them,

> You go, and say to that fox, Look, I put
> out demons and will send healings today and
> tomorrow, and on the third day I will be
> completed. Except that I must go today and
> tomorrow and the following day, because a
> prophet cannot perish outside of Jerusalem!
> (Luke 13:31–33)

There are several indications that we are dealing with
primitive material here. The Pharisees are friendly, it is
assumed that Herod is particularly interested in miracles, and the Lukan Jesus does not speak in his usual,
precise way about how and when he is going to die. In-
stead, Yeshua puts himself into the general category of
prophets who will be killed as a result of their prophecy.

What the saying shows us is that Yeshua's geographical program avoided Herod Antipas, and that it did so
deliberately until such time as confrontation with authorities might take place. And the only place for that
was Jerusalem.

The Politics of Purity

Yohanan's program of generic immersion assumed that
Israel, and even those in Samaria, could be made pure.

God's provision of living water in the Jordan Valley, the entry point of Joshua into the land of promise, made for the reconstitution of Israel in that place. At this point, it seems appropriate to mention that Yeshua's name was the Aramaic equivalent of Joshua (Yehoshua in Hebrew). Having a follower so named is not likely to have escaped Yohanan. The possibility of the fulfillment of promise was redolent from the very beginning.

To the extent that the narrative of Yeshua's immersion may reflect his own orientation, that fulfillment seems to be carried on. Now it must be stressed that that extent is limited. The story of Yeshua's immersion in the Synoptic Gospels is a model of the primitive experience of Christian baptism as it came to be practiced after the resurrection.[18] That marked the moment when, as we will see in the last chapter, Yeshua's movement stressed the availability of the spirit for every believer in order to fulfill the covenant of Israel, and the preaching became increasingly international, and predominantly Greek. Yeshua became Jesus; his movement became Christianity. Christian catechumens, prepared by a year-long catechesis such as the Gospel according to Mark represents, enter the water and are able to call on God as father under the inspiration of the holy spirit, which is Jesus' own spirit (see Gal. 4:4–6). Believers can call God father because the same spirit informs the believers that they are God's sons and daughters (as in

---

18. See Bruce Chilton and Jacob Neusner, *Jewish-Christian Debates: God, Kingdom, Messiah* (Minneapolis: Fortress, 1998), 62–66.

Mark 1:11). The dialectics of the spirit, such that it is poured out to enable the relationship between father and son as the truth of the covenant, was what permitted Christianity to thrive as a religious movement despite its lack of the usual resources (material, social, and historical) which make for the emergence of a major religion.

That theology, which represents the fundamentals of Christianity, obviously cannot be attributed to Yohanan, although — as we have seen in chapter 1 — that has been the tendency of interpreters, to make Yohanan the first saint of Christianity. But having said that, it would be odd if the story of Jesus' immersion in the Synoptic Gospels represented nothing whatever about Yohanan. After all, the Synoptics are contemporaneous with Josephus, and we have been willing to consider his description of Yohanan, provided we allow for his thematic biases. Can we not proceed in the same way with the Synoptics?

The way forward in just this direction was shown by K. Chamblin in an article that appeared more than thirty-five years ago in the *Tyndale House Bulletin*.[19] He considered and developed the observation that Yohanan is rightly to be conceived, in his own terms, not as the forerunner of Yeshua/Jesus, but as the forerunner of God. There is a bit of irony here. While the

---

19. K. Chamblin, "Gospel and Judgment in the Preaching of John the Baptist," *Tyndale House Bulletin* 13 (1963): 7–15; see also J. H. Hughes, "John the Baptist: The Forerunner of God Himself," *New Testament Studies* 14 (1972): 191–218.

Jesus Seminar has been reputed as being hypercritical, it has continued to portray Yohanan as the prophet of Yeshua/Jesus, while it was an evangelical scholar who more clearly sets out a critical orientation. The received opinion, which makes all evangelicals credulous and all members of the Jesus Seminar skeptics, is in need of education.

The key to Yohanan's preparation for God himself lies in the wording attributed to him, "I immerse you in water, but he himself will immerse you in holy spirit" (Mark 1:8; see Matt. 3:11 and Luke 3:16). Outside the context of Christianity, where those words are fulfilled by what the risen Jesus endows the believer with, only God himself can give of his own spirit. Indeed, the link between purification with water and the vindicating presence of God's spirit is explicitly made in the book of Ezekiel:

> Therefore, say to the house of Israel: So says the Lord, the LORD: Not for your sake am I acting, house of Israel, but for my holy name, which you have profaned among the peoples you came to. I will sanctify my great name, although profaned among the peoples among whom you have profaned it, and the peoples will know that I am the LORD, says the Lord, the LORD, when I am sanctified among you before their eyes. I will take you from the peoples, and gather you from all the lands, and bring you to your land. I will sprinkle on you clean waters and cleanse you from all your unclean-

nesses and from all your idols I will cleanse you. I will give you a new heart and a new spirit I will put in your midst, and remove the heart of stone from your flesh and give you a heart of flesh. My spirit I shall put in your midst and I will make you walk according to my statutes and keep my judgments and do them. (Ezek. 36:22–27)

The close and causal connection between water and spirit here has led to the suggestion that we have at hand an important scriptural precedent of Yohanan's immersion.[20] The usage of similar imagery in the *Rule of the Community* from Qumran (1QS 4.19–23) and in *Jubilees* (1:22–25) has been described by Lars Harman as "a sounding board for the appearance of John the Baptist."[21]

The response is readily made, of course, that these words from Ezekiel are not actually cited in association with Yohanan anywhere. Josephus does not provide him with any scriptural program, and the Gospels invoke the imagery of Isaiah (which appears to have been Yeshua's favorite book, in the form of the Aramaic Targum[22]). The

---

20. See Otto Böcher, "Johannes der Täufer," *Theologische Real-enzyklopädie* 17 (1988): 175.

21. Lars Hartman, *"Into the Name of the Lord Jesus": Baptism in the Early Church,* Studies of the New Testament and Its World (Edinburgh: Clark, 1997), 12.

22. See Bruce Chilton, *A Galilean Rabbi and His Bible: Jesus' Use of the Interpreted Scripture of His Time* (Wilmington: Glazier, 1984); also published with the subtitle *Jesus' Own Interpretation of Isaiah* (London: SPCK, 1984).

discipline of the study of the New Testament, however, sometimes poses questions in too binary a fashion. In this case: did Yohanan cite Ezekiel or did he not? There is no reason to assume that Yohanan or Yeshua was literate. Insofar as Yeshua knew Isaiah, for example, it seems to have been in the form of an Aramaic paraphrase which was oral in his time, and his own reference to it was remarkably free. The idea that one needs a Scripture to follow a religious impulse is not the rule in the study of religions. By the same token, the fact that the citation of a specific Scripture cannot be demonstrated does not rule out the possibility that Scriptures may inform us in regard to the religious milieu in which people act.

In the present case, the passage from Ezekiel links purifying water and God's spirit. It also invokes ideas of sanctification and righteousness, which Josephus associates with Yohanan, and themes of judgment and the promise of the land pledged to Israel, which the Synoptic Gospels associate with him. All those connections still do not prove that Yohanan cited Ezekiel, and that is not the suggestion here. But they do suggest that Ezekiel represents a classic expression of the hope of restoration from exile which was taken up by Yohanan (much as in the *Rule of the Community* and in *Jubilees*) in his own program of cleansing by immersion.[23]

Pursuing his program around the Jordan, reminiscent of Joshua's triumphant crossing into the land of prom-

---

23. For discussion of a theology of restoration, see E. P. Sanders, *Jesus and Judaism* (Philadelphia: Fortress, 1985), 77–119.

ise, Yohanan articulated the meaning of his immersion
with great precision. Just that makes us pause when we
consider Yeshua's move into Galilean villages. The motivation of his act from the point of view of the threat
of Herod Antipas is easily enough understood. But if
Yeshua followed Yohanan, accepted and administered his
immersion, and himself bore the name of Joshua, how
could he have distanced himself from the geographical
aspect of Yohanan's symbolism? How, in fact, could he
have just stopped immersing people altogether?

The implications of Yeshua's radical departure from
Yohanan's program will concern us in a moment. First,
we need to consider the basis on which he felt empow-
ered to depart as radically as he did. Within the same
narrative of his immersion which we have been referring to, it is said that Yeshua saw a vision of a dove and
heard a voice. Those are the marks of his reception of
the spirit of God.

Where the spirit was for Yohanan the means by which
God accomplished the righteousness and purification of
his people, and where for primitive Christianity the spirit
was an outpouring through Jesus for all believers in Jesus,
for Yeshua himself it was something else. We can better
understand his own experience by reference to a story
about another rabbi and the holy spirit.

The story concerns an older contemporary of Yeshua,
Hillel, whose links with Yeshua's actions have already
concerned us.[24] In the expanded edition of the Mish-

---

24. See Bruce Chilton, *Jesus' Prayer and Jesus' Eucharist: His*

nah known as the Tosefta, from the third century C.E., we read:

> Until the dead live — namely, Haggai, Zecha-riah, and Malachi, the latter prophets [who were thought to have remained alive with God][25] — the holy spirit has ceased from Israel. The sages were gathered at the house of Guria in Jericho, and they heard a *bat qol* [an echo from heaven] saying,
>
> > There is here a man who is predestined for the holy spirit, except that his generation is not righteous for such.
>
> And they put their eyes on Hillel the elder, and when he died, they said of him,
>
> > Woe the meek man, Woe the faithful disciple of Ezra. (Sotah 13:3)[26]

Yeshua's immersion in Mark also refers to the sound of a heavenly echo, a "daughter of a voice" in Hebrew, but in addition Yeshua's own vision, of the heavens opening and the spirit descending, is a distinctive trait.

Personal Practice of Spirituality (Valley Forge, Pa.: Trinity Press International, 1997), 65–69.

25. In the Talmud (Megillah 3a), for example, it is claimed, "The Targum of the Prophets was composed by Jonathan ben Uzziel under the guidance of Haggai, Zechariah and Malachi," although Jonathan lived long after the time of those prophets.

26. See the full discussion in Bruce Chilton, *Profiles of a Rabbi: Synoptic Opportunities in Reading about Jesus*, Brown Judaic Studies 177 (Atlanta: Scholars Press, 1989), 77–89.

It has been argued by Ulrich Müller, Stephen Gero, and Joel Marcus[27] that the visionary emphases of the scene of Yeshua's immersion, along with his statement concerning Satan falling from heaven (Luke 10:18) and the Transfiguration (Matt. 17:1–9; Mark 9:2–10; Luke 9:28–36), reflect characteristics of his own experience. The testimony of vision appears to have been interpreted by him as the authorization of God's spirit. The result was that the tradition concerning Yeshua took just the turn which the tradition concerning Hillel did not. Yeshua's own vision of the dove as the spirit[28] radically changed his orientation and his conception of purity. As Joan Taylor has shown, reference to Yeshua as "son" and as "beloved" accords with his understanding that the spirit of God had descended on him. She cites the examples of Honi the Circler, who compared himself to a son standing before God (Mishnah Taanit 3:8) and of Daniel being addressed as a "beloved man" (Dan.

---

27. See Ulrich Müller, "Vision und Botschaft: Erwägungen zur prophetischen Struktur der Verkündigung Jesus," *Zeitschrift für Theologie und Kirche* 74 (1977): 416–48; Stephen Gero, "The Spirit as a Dove in the Baptism of Jesus," *Novum Testamentum* 18 (1976): 17–35; Joel Marcus, "Jesus' Baptismal Vision," *New Testament Studies* 41 (1995): 512–21. As Marcus's title implies, he transposes the *vision of Satan* falling into the scene of the baptism, a move for which I see no exegetical reason or interpretative advantage. Nonetheless, his observation of the similar structure of the assertion of the two visions is helpful.

28. For a recent discussion (supplementing Gero's contribution), see Dale C. Allison, "The Baptism of Jesus and a New Dead Sea Scroll," *Biblical Archeology Review* (1992): 58–60.

10:11).[29] Yeshua's move into Galilee, then, was not only political in the sense that it was convenient. It also represents the moment at which Yeshua ceased to prepare Israel for God's coming in the manner of Yohanan, but announced as his personal message that God was now in the very process of coming. The prophet Haggai had spoken of God's spirit as that which was in Israel and enabled Israel to be holy, despite its uncleanness (see Hag. 2:4, 10–19). So now Yeshua taught his disciples to sanctify God's name and welcome God's kingdom in a regular discipline of prayer.[30]

The meal served for Yeshua from Galilee onward in much the same way that immersion had served for Yohanan (and Yeshua) before that time. Pharisaic constructions of purity had demanded that only those who practiced cleanness and paid tithe could be accepted in fellowship and could offer fellowship. In the tractate Demai 2:2–3 in the Mishnah, someone who was suspected of not paying tithe could not invite a faithful Israelite home for a meal. Invited to a meal among the faithful, such a person would first need to change clothing. Yeshua taught that the act of fellowship at meals created an instance of Israel which celebrated the

---

29. Joan E. Taylor, *The Immerser: John the Baptist within Second Temple Judaism,* Studying the Historical Jesus 2 (Grand Rapids: Eerdmans, 1997), 269–77. On that basis, she attributes a self-consciously prophetic identity to Yeshua, which in my opinion is not a sound inference.

30. The aspects of Jesus' prayer which contribute to its distinctiveness; see *Jesus' Prayer and Jesus' Eucharist,* 32–38.

kingdom of God in advance; the forgiveness and the generosity practiced there were the seal of God's impending triumph. His behavior might be compared, not to Yohanan's, but to that of Ma'yan, the tax agent who is praised in the Talmud Yerushalmi (Hagigah 2:2) for giving a meal for the poor in Askalon.[31] Only his conviction that his actions were warranted by God's spirit adequately explains why Yeshua would not only depart from Yohanan's program of immersing, but announce God's kingdom by means of his practice, and his disciples' practice, of fellowship at meals in Galilee.

Naturally, Yeshua's own program ultimately had to include the Temple, that holy place where, according to Haggai, God's spirit had prepared a focus of sanctity for God. Yeshua's vision of Israel involved forgiveness and gifts in kind at meals, such as the rural Galilee he knew could provide for. That Israel, that purity, that sacrifice were unlike the urban system of sacrifice in Jerusalem, which had become based more on currency. Yeshua's occupation of the Temple, including his citation of the prophet Zechariah, represents his final insistence on a politics of purity unlike Yohanan's, the practice of welcoming God as already regnant rather than of preparing for God's coming.[32]

---

31. See Fritz Herrenbrück, *Jesus und die Zöllner: Historische und neutestamentlich-exegetische Untersuchungen,* Wissenschaftliche Untersuchungen zum Neuen Testament 41 (Tübingen: Mohr, 1990), 213–16.

32. Again, see Chilton, *Jesus' Prayer and Jesus' Eucharist,* 7–23, 59–75.

Conclusion: The Identification of Yohanan with Elijah

In order to mark out his own program in contrast to Yohanan's, Yeshua developed a theological evaluation of Yohanan. Famously, he compared him to Elijah and drew from the book of Malachi (3:1) in order to do so (Luke 7:27–28; Matt. 11:10–11; see also Mark 1:2):

This is he concerning whom it was written,

> Look, I send my messenger before your face,
> who will prepare your way before you.

I say to you, among those born of women there is not one greater than Yohanan. But the least in the kingdom of God is greater than he.

Within Rabbinic tradition, Haggai, Zechariah, and Malachi were linked as deathless figures (as in the story about Hillel discussed earlier). They concerned God's final preparation by his spirit (so the book of Haggai) of a purified and inclusive Temple (so the book of Zechariah) for which a people was to be readied by Elijah (so the book of Malachi).

The statement about Yohanan seems unambiguous, and the identification of him with Malachi's Elijah (Mal. 4:5) makes him *the* prophet "before the great and terrible day of the LORD comes." But when that day arrives, when it is a matter of God's kingdom in itself approaching, Yohanan's role is already a matter of history. Two contrasts between Yohanan and Yeshua, expressible by means of reference to Malachi, underscore this point. First, the continuation of the prophecy of the messenger in Malachi 3:1 speaks of when "the Lord whom you seek will suddenly come to his Temple." That role cannot plausibly be applied to Yohanan, but it suits Yeshua's action in the Temple, and it may be echoed in Yohanan's question to him, "Are you the one who comes, or do we anticipate another?" (see Matt. 11:3; Luke 7:19). Second, Malachi closes with the function of Elijah, as being to "turn the hearts of the fathers to their children and the hearts of the children to their fathers" (Mal. 4:6). Yeshua's function is so neatly opposite in much teaching attributed to him (see Matt. 10:21; Mark 13:12; Luke 21:16; Matt. 19:28–29; Mark 10:29–30) that a contrast with the stance of Yohanan seems implicit.

Yohanan the immerser became Elijah the prophet first within the theology of Yeshua, who made his own rabbi the precursor of the purity which he saw being realized by God in the fellowship of the kingdom within Israel.

~ 3 ~

Purification and Healing in the Ministry of Yeshua

Cleansing, Restoring in the Program of Yeshua

The Synoptic Gospels agree in presenting the story of what is commonly known as Yeshua's cleansing of a "leper" early in their portrayals of his ministry (Matt. 8:2–4; Mark 1:40–44; Luke 5:12–14). This story is a model of what the healing of Yeshua involved. A "leper" approaches Yeshua, and — for no stated reason — asserts that Yeshua is able to "cleanse" him. That cleansing, as we are about to see in some detail, involves a finding that the man is pure, and that — consequently — he may be restored to fellowship with Israel, even to the point of offering sacrifice in the Temple. Yeshua agrees, pronouncing the man clean and ordering him to show himself to a priest, and then to offer the sacrifice prescribed by Moses for cleansing.

What comes to be translated "leprosy" in the Bible is not the direct equivalent of the disease caused by what is called Hansen's bacillus, leading to the terrible results which are widely known. The term in Hebrew (*sara'at*) would better be rendered "outbreak" and refers to the broken condition of skin in humans — or, for that matter, walls in houses. (The description in Leviticus, chapters 13 and 14, makes it plain that a large number of causes and conditions could have brought about an "outbreak" of skin or wall.[1]) The threat of the condition is that it breaks boundaries, so that people come into contact with what makes them impure. That is the case whether the impurity is from the blood under human skin or from anything outside of a house from which the wall might provide protection. "Outbreak," unlike Hansen's disease, comes and goes, and Leviticus makes it a priestly duty to detect its presence and absence.

If a person is declared clean by a priest, two different offerings are required in Leviticus 14. The first is a local sacrifice and may take place wherever there is running water. The priest kills a bird in an earthen vessel over the water and dips a living bird in the dead one's blood, having beforehand attached cedar, scarlet, and hyssop to the living bird. He then sprinkles the sufferer from "outbreak" with the living bird and releases it (14:1–8).[2] Purification follows (see v. 9), after which

---

1. I once asked a colleague who is trained in biology how the combination of symptoms might be regarded from a medical point of view. He referred to several conditions in humans which might correspond to the diagnosis of "outbreak," but observed that the attribution of "outbreak" to walls took it outside the purview of medical diagnosis as we know it.

2. It seems clear that the end of sacrifice is to separate the per-

the sufferer needs to offer two male lambs, a ewe, cereal, and oil; together they constitute a sacrifice for guilt, a sacrifice for sin, a burnt sacrifice, and a cereal sacrifice, all with the sufferer particularly in view (14:10–20). Exceptional provisions are made for instances of poverty (vv. 21–32), but the requirement of ownership remains onerous within the provisions in Leviticus.

The story concerning Yeshua therefore refers to a specific moment in the process of purification. The sufferer from "outbreak" attributes to Yeshua the ability to determine the status of his skin, and Yeshua accepts the responsibility of telling him he may proceed *directly* to the sacrificial moment which ordinarily is to occur after cleanness has been declared. Although Yeshua is not portrayed as taking over any sacrificial function, he is explicitly assigned — within the terms of reference the story itself establishes — the authority to pronounce on matters of purity in the way that a local priest might.

Yeshua himself appears to have been keenly concerned with purity as such. The animating assumption in Yeshua's cleansing of the man with "outbreak" is that purity is not merely a function of diagnosis by observation. An entire tractate of the Mishnah, called Nega'im, is devoted to the issue, how skin might be investigated and treated (by means including surgery) in the interests of declaring a person free of "outbreak." That perspective

son from the impurity. On the role of separation within certain types of sacrifice, see Bruce Chilton, *The Temple of Jesus: His Sacrificial Program within a Cultural History of Sacrifice* (University Park: Pennsylvania State University Press, 1992), 27–42.

in the Mishnah, which was composed in its present form c. 200 c.e., reflects at least one of the views of purity current among Pharisees during the first century. Yeshua sets up another perspective: the integrity of the skin comes from the integrity underneath the skin. Yeshua holds in the story that the determinative factor is the man's approach in the expectation of purity and Yeshua's agreement to the purification. The Psalms bring to open expression the regular association of righteousness and purity (see 18:21 [v. 20 in English versions]; 24:3–6; 26:4–7; 51:4, 8, 9, 12 [English vv. 2, 6, 7, 10]; 119:9), and Yeshua insisted that the wholeness of those two also made for purity and — therefore — healing.

The link between such integrity and cleanness is explicitly made when Yeshua asserts:

> There is nothing outside a person entering in that can defile, but what comes out of a person is what defiles a person. (Mark 7:15; Matt. 15:11)

This is no denial here of the importance of purity as such.[3] The issue is rather the *direction* from which purity might proceed. Yeshua's claim is that observances of purity do not create the reality, but that human acts and words might extend the claim of the pure, as in the case

---

3. The context of the statement in Mark 7 makes the overall topic the purity of foods, but that was obviously not the generative concern of Yeshua: his meaning is not limited to what goes in and what goes out of a person in that sense; see Bruce Chilton, "A Generative Exegesis of Mark 7:1–23," *Journal of Higher Criticism* 3, no. 1 (1996): 18–37.

of the man with "outbreak." Purity is the condition in which an Israelite lives as an Israelite, not an achievement of practice or observation. Purity for Yeshua is less a status to be attained than a power which cleanses.

The point of such sayings as Matthew 15:11, Mark 7:15, and the story of the cleansing of the man with "outbreak" is that Israelites are properly understood as pure and that what extends from a person, what a person is and does and has, manifests that purity. Health for Yeshua comes from that wholeness, and from an awareness of that wholeness. It is not so much the elimination of disease as it is the working outward of the integrity of Israel as provided by God. The cultural distance between us and the "leper" in the story makes it impossible for us to say clinically what the man was suffering from or what he looked like before and after his cleansing by Yeshua. But that is just Yeshua's point: our integrity is not a matter of symptoms, but our acceptance of how God wants us to be.

Hillel has already been mentioned (in chapter 2, pp. 51–53) as offering a useful comparison with the conception of Yeshua's relationship to the spirit. In the present case, a more direct comparison with the understanding that purity extends from an Israelite may be offered. Hillel defended an Israelite's right to enter a Roman bath on the grounds that, if non-Jews deem it an honor to wash the idols of their gods, Israelites should take on the devotion of washing their bodies, which bear the very image of God (see Leviticus Rabbah 34.3). Bathing here does not make one pure, but celebrates the fact of purity.

The similarity with Yeshua's teaching is striking, especially because what is attributed to Hillel is actually more heterodox than the teaching attributed to Yeshua in the Gospels. After all, Yeshua is merely stating the direction in which purity is to be understood to develop; Hillel is validating the practice of bathing in the manner of the Romans. A kindred idea is also attributed to Paul (who described himself as a Pharisee in Phil. 3:5), although he expressed it more stolidly, "Do you not know that your body is a temple of the holy spirit within you, which you have from God?" (1 Cor. 6:19). All three teachers, Hillel, Paul, and Yeshua, assume that cleanness is at base an issue of integrity. All three assert that the divine presence within a person (the image of God for Hillel, purity for Yeshua, the holy spirit for Paul) assures that the Israelite is to be seen as clean and, by definition, acceptable to God.

But Yeshua *is* unusual in his behaving as if purity were contagious. Just as he sent disciples out to encounter rural Galilee as pure Israel,[4] so his encounter with the man with "outbreak" is assumed to heal the "outbreak." Clearly, the Markan narrative of this healing is closely linked with the theme that Yeshua was able to exorcise unclean spirits (see Mark 1:23–28, 32–34), and the tiny vignette involving the healing of Peter's mother-in-law also precedes (1:29–31). Those connections need to be explored as part of the wider issue of the "signs" with which Yeshua's activities were associated. But the en-

---

4. See Chilton, *Jesus' Prayer and Jesus' Eucharist*, 4–6, 16–18.

counter of Yeshua with the man with "outbreak" sets up a deliberate, direct, and emphatic link between healing and purification.

A famous saying of Yeshua's in Mark sets up the connection quite plainly:

> Those who are healthy have no need of a physician, but those who are ill; I have not come to call the righteous, but sinners. (Mark 2:17)

"Sinners" are essentially those with whom contact is prohibited or restricted. It has been argued that they are to be seen as the "wicked" (*rasha'*) of early Judaic and Rabbinic literature and subject to final punishment as such, but it seems more plausible to associate them with the "sinners" (*ḥa'ev*, the indebted) who are called to repent from what they do.[5] Yeshua's point is that bringing them into fellowship with Israel results in their healing. He is the physician of contagious purity.

Two passages are especially redolent of the same perspective, but in the medium of action rather than of words. In Mark 5:21–43, Yeshua enters into contact with the two primary sources of impurity, blood and death, and purifies them both. The association of the two stories — and their two media of impurity — cannot be coincidental, because the narrative of the woman with a flow of blood is sandwiched within the story of the raising of Yair's daughter:

---

5. The former judgment is that of E. P. Sanders; the latter is my own. See Bruce Chilton, "Jesus and the Repentance of E. P. Sanders," *Tyndale Bulletin* 39 (1988): 1–18.

²²And one of the leaders of the synagogues comes, named Yair. He sees him and falls at his feet, ²³ and implores him a lot, saying,

> My little daughter is at her end, so come lay hands on her, so she might be saved and live.

²⁴And he went after him, and a big crowd followed him and pressed in on him. ²⁵And a woman who had a flow of blood twelve years ²⁶ (and had suffered a lot from many physicians and had spent everything she had and was no better but rather got worse) ²⁷ heard concerning Yeshua. She came in the crowd from behind, and touched his garment. ²⁸ For she said,

> If I touch even his garments, I will be saved.

²⁹And at once the fountain of her blood dried up, and she knew in her body that she was healed of her illness. ³⁰ Yeshua at once recognized in himself the power gone out of him, turned in the crowd, and said,

> Who touched me?

³¹And his students said to him,

> You see the crowed pressing in on you, and you ask, Who touched me?

³²And he looked around to see the woman who had done it. ³³ But the woman was afraid and trembling: she knew what had happened to her. She came and

fell before him and told him the whole truth. ³⁴ But he said to her,

> Daughter, your faith has saved you; depart in peace and be healed from your illness.

³⁵ While he was still speaking, they come from the leader of the synagogue, saying,

> Your little daughter is dead: why do you still bother the teacher?

³⁶ But Yeshua overheard the word spoken, and says to the leader of the synagogue,

> Do not be afraid; only believe.

³⁷And he did not let anyone follow along with him except Rock and Yakob and Yohanan the brother of Yakob. ³⁸And they come into the house of the leader of the synagogue, and he sees a disturbance, both weeping and much wailing, ³⁹ and he entered and says to them,

> Why are you distressed and weeping? The child is not dead, but sleeps.

⁴⁰And they ridiculed him. But he put everyone out, takes the father of the child and the mother and those with him and goes into where the child was. ⁴¹ He grasped the hand of the child and he says to her, *Talitha kuoum*, which is translated:

> Girl, I say to you, arise.

[42]And at once the girl arose and walked around, for she was twelve years old. And they were at once beside themselves with great excitement. [43]And he admonished them a lot so that no one should know this, and he said to give her something to eat.

In addition to the fact that one story is sandwiched within the other,[6] the woman had the flow of blood for twelve years, Yair's daughter was twelve years old, they are both called "daughter," and — of course — they are both women. It would be difficult to construct a story more pointed toward the issue of purity, and the relationship to the issue of healing is manifest.

The intensity of focus on purity is also manifest in the relationship between the two types of uncleanness involved. Yair's daughter is thought to be dead, and a corpse is a primary source of contagious uncleanness: it is the way a being is not created by God. In the book of Haggai, the prophet asks the question of the priests whether contact with a holy thing makes a thing holy and permits it to communicate holiness further. They answer "no," but they readily agree that the contact with a corpse makes whatever touches it unclean, and also that uncleanness by indirect contact results (Hag. 2:11–13). Haggai underscores, then, the intense conviction that corpses communicate uncleanness. The woman in

---

6. For a discussion of this technique within Mark and further discussion (with bibliography) see Joanna Dewey, "The Literary Structure of the Controversy Stories in Mark 2:-3:6," *Journal of Biblical Literature* 92, no. 3 (1981): 394–401.

the story, however, is a source of blood; the uncleanness associated with her is of a different order. Blood does not belong to the realm of human contact because "the blood is the life" (Lev. 17:10–13; Deut. 12:23), and contact with menstruating women or women with irregular bleeding is a matter of systematic control (Lev. 15:19–30). Death and blood are the longitude and latitude of maps of purity, and these two stories together seek to redraw that map.

The task of mapping purity and impurity is, of course, also taken up in Mishnah, which devotes a tractate to observing how corpse-uncleanness (as well as other impurities) may be determined and how far it extends (Ohalot), and a tractate to the questions of flows such as the woman had (Zabim), and — for that matter — a tractate to how to diagnose and treat "outbreak" (Nega'im). What is stunning about the stories in Mark within the context of Judaism is not the fact that impurity is recognized, but its treatment. How we are to account for the flow of blood stopping and the girl reviving is not explained, except on the confidence that Yeshua's purification amounts to healing. Contagious purity is also healing purity.

The direction of purity then, from the inside out, is consistent as one compares such stories with Yeshua's distinctive teaching. Mention has already been made of the question posed by the prophet Haggai, whose point is that — normally speaking — it is uncleanness that is contagious, not sanctity. But the larger point is that, because God's spirit is active within Israel (Hag. 2:5), despite the current state of uncleanness, the Temple can be sanctified, blessing will come, the line of David is continued (Hag. 2:14–23). Yeshua's point is similar, but it is directed to the body of Israel rather than to the body of the Temple. Moreover, he holds that healing purification may be generalized, to the extent that he sends some of his disciples to heal in the name of the kingdom of God (see Luke 10:9; Matt. 10:7–8; Mark 6:13; Luke 9:6).

Just as Mark's stories of healing model the systemic link with purification, so they portray how contagious purity is to be mediated. Indeed, that is done just after the story of the man with "outbreak":

> [1] He entered again into Kapharnaum for days and it was heard that he was in house. [2] And many were gathered, with the result that there was no longer room to move, even by the door, and he talked the word to them. [3] And they come carrying a paraplegic to him, borne by four. [4] They were not able to carry through to him because of the crowd, and they unroofed the roof where he was, and digging up, they lower the litter where the paraplegic was lying. [5] Yeshua sees their faith, and says to the paraplegic,

> Child, your sins have been released.

> [6] But some of the judges were sitting there and deliberating in their hearts,

> [7] Is he talking like this? He is cursing! Who is able to release sins except one — God!

[8]At once Yeshua recognizes in his spirit that they were deliberating among themselves and says,

> Why are you deliberating these things in your hearts? [9] What is easier, to say to the paraplegic, your sins are released, or so say — rise, and take up your litter and walk? [10] But so that you may know that the son of man has authority to release sins upon the earth, he says to the paraplegic, [11] to you I say, Rise, take up your litter and depart into your house.

[12]And he arose and at once taking up the litter, he went out before all, with the result that all were beside themselves and glorified God,

> We have never seen this. (Mark 2:1–12)

Once that strong connection has been made between forgiveness and healing, it colors the stories of healing which follow.

Prayer for forgiveness on a regular basis was a distinctive feature of the model of prayer Yeshua developed, and within that model there is a structural connection between forgiveness and the sanctification of God's name.[7] Forgiveness and sanctity are linked, and now we can see that both are related strongly to purification and healing. The sanctifying presence of God in Israel, referred to as God's spirit by Haggai and seen at his immersion by Yeshua, is made known when Israel

---

7. See Chilton, *Jesus' Prayer and Jesus' Eucharist.*

is forgiven. And that holiness is contagious: it purifies and heals.

The Contagion of Purity in Yeshua's Practice

Yeshua's perception of the spirit of God at his own immersion by Yohanan, then, is related directly and causally to his practice of purification and healing. A fragment concerning the messiah recently discovered in the cave numbered four at Qumran makes the connection between the messiah, the spirit, healing, and purity:

> The heavens and the earth will obey his messiah.
> ...Over the meek his spirit will hover, and the faithful he will restore by his power. He will glorify the pious ones on the throne of the eternal kingdom. He will release the captives, make the blind see, raise up the downtrodden....Then he will heal the slain, resurrect the dead, and announce glad tidings to the poor.[8]

As Craig Evans has pointed out, this passage illuminates the activity and the self-understanding of Yeshua. When the Gospels portray Yohanan as sending out from prison to Yeshua, asking whether he is the one who is to come,

---

8. For the text and a discussion, see Craig A. Evans, "Jesus and the Dead Sea Scrolls from Qumran Cave 4," *Eschatology, Messianism, and the Dead Sea Scrolls,* Studies in the Dead Sea Scrolls and Related Literature 1, ed. C. A. Evans and P. W. Flint (Grand Rapids: Eerdmans, 1997), 96–97.

Yeshua replies, "Go, announce to Yohanan what you have seen and heard, blind people see again, lame people walk about, people with outbreak are cleansed, deaf people hear, dead are raised, poor people have victory heralded (Matt. 11:4–5; Luke 7:22). Evans concentrates on the reference to the dead being raised. The list of activities Yeshua mentions are, on the whole, found as part of the prophetic announcement in the book of Isaiah (see Isa. 35:5–6; 61:1–2), but there is no reference to the dead being raised in that context. Because the fragment from Qumran does make that reference, Evans argues convincingly that it informs us of the sort of messianic conception which influenced Yeshua.[9]

That reference to raising the dead is evidently important here, as is the reference to the spirit. Together, they show us that the activities referred to in Isaiah 35:5–6 and the mention of God's spirit in Isaiah 61:1 were already associated in messianic terms by the time Yeshua cited them. Further, and more obviously, the passage "supports the traditional view that Jesus did indeed see himself as Israel's Messiah."[10] But the fragment has still more to teach us. Because it is a fragment, the absence

---

9. As he points out in agreement with my earlier work, p. 97 n. 14, the prophetic message is especially similar to the Targum of Isaiah, which explicitly mentions the kingdom of God. See Bruce Chilton, *God in Strength: Jesus' Announcement of the Kingdom,* Studien zum Neuen Testament und seiner Umwelt 1 (Freistadt: Plöchl, 1979); reprinted in *The Biblical Seminar* (Sheffield: JSOT, 1987), 277–93.

10. See Evans, "Jesus and the Dead Sea Scrolls from Qumran Cave 4," 97.

of any reference to healing those with "outbreak" — to which Yeshua refers in Matthew and Luke, but the book of Isaiah does not — might conceivably be accidental. At any rate, we are in no position to claim that Yeshua was somehow unique in associating cleaning outbreak with the other activities mentioned.

Yeshua is also portrayed as citing Isaiah 61 in the Gospel according to Luke (chapter 4). Yeshua travels to Nazareth, where he was brought up, and goes to synagogue on the Sabbath, as was his habit. He is given a scroll containing the book of Isaiah, in accordance with the regular practice of that congregation (Luke 4:15–17). So far everything that happens is predictable and routine. (Indeed, that only needs emphasizing because some scholars have encouraged us to forget or to marginalize Yeshua's Judaism.) But then there is an odd turn in the events, and the oddity concerns Yeshua's retelling of Scripture. For his reading is no simple reading, but a transforming of the book of Isaiah. He says,

> The spirit of the Lord is upon me,
> because he has anointed me
> to announce news of triumph to the poor.
> He has sent me to preach release to prisoners,
> and renewal of sight to the blind,
> to send the oppressed into release,
> to preach the acceptable year of the Lord.

Once Yeshua has said this, people stare at him, and finally they reject what he says. What is the surprise? What is the offense?

First, Yeshua's "reading" is no reading. He here drops a phrase from the chapter of Isaiah (61:1–2) and adds one of his own, a phrase that speaks of giving renewal of sight to the blind. Reference to the blind in Aramaic of the period of Yeshua often refers to those who do not see the meaning of the Torah, and that is the sense of the expression here. In fact, the Aramaic paraphrase of Isaiah, the Targum of Isaiah, takes the imagery of blindness just that way in Isaiah 35:5. Yeshua is saying that, in retelling Scripture, he is making the meaning of Scripture clear to those who are blind.

The reason for surprise and growing opposition in the synagogue becomes apparent, especially when Yeshua goes on to say, "Today this Scripture is fulfilled in your ears" (Luke 4:21). He claims to speak in the ears of the congregation in the interests of opening their eyes.

Whether Yeshua cited Scripture or told parables of his own invention, the purpose was the same. He framed a particular argument, characteristic of his message and of Christianity ever since. He claimed that God's power could be perceived as a kingdom, and that the kingdom of God was the basis on which our lives could be transformed. You could see it in the book of Isaiah or in mustard seed (for example), but whether in a text or in a field the point of the kingdom of God was that it needed to be acknowledged and joined in order to be entered.

The field in which a seed grows changes with the growth. A text in which the kingdom is experienced is also transformed. Isaiah is different as a result of being retold in the interests of the kingdom: the text could be changed, and was changed, and Yeshua insisted on changing it. Not just here, but time and again, he cites the book of Isaiah and other texts in forms which are not attested in Hebrew or Greek or Aramaic. To some extent, that is because he was a popular rabbi, perhaps even illiterate, but that is only part of the reason. The more profound cause was that, in the vision of Jesus, the kingdom changed the way you saw the text, just as it changed the way you saw nature and people.

Within the context of Yeshua's reference to Isaiah in Luke 4, in which Yeshua's connection with the spirit of God is especially developed, we also discover the partic- ular association of that spirit with cleansing people from "outbreak." Following his citation of his own version of Isaiah 61, Yeshua goes on, by way of precedent for his own activity, to give the example of Elisha (Luke 4:27). Within the Lukan presentation, the emphasis of the ex- ample falls on the fact that the person whom Elisha cleansed of "outbreak" was a Syrian, and as non-Jewish as possible (in 2 Kings 5). That is not likely to have been Yeshua's point, but the fact of the link between Elisha and cleaning from "outbreak" remains. And the Hebrew Bible is quite clear why Elisha was endowed with such powers:

And Elijah took his cloak and rolled it up and struck the waters and they were divided to each side, and the two of them passed over on dry ground. And it happened when they had passed over, Elijah said to Elisha, "Request what I should

do for you before I am taken from you." Elisha
said, "May twice your spirit become mine." He
said, "You made a hard request! If you see me taken
from you, it shall be yours, and if not, it will not
be." As they went on walking and talking, look:
a chariot of fire and horses of fire! They parted
the two of them, and Elijah went up by a whirl-
wind of heaven. Elisha saw, and he cried out, "My
father, my father — the chariot of Israel and its
horses!" He did not see him any more, and he tore
his clothes, and ripped the pieces in two.

(2 Kings 2:8–12)

Elisha's particular abilities, including his healing of Naa-
man, a Syrian general, from "outbreak," are the result
of his endowment with the spirit that was also Elijah's.
When Yeshua claimed that the spirit of God is upon
him, it was natural for him to associate the cleansing of
those with "outbreak" with that endowment.

We have already seen (in chapter 2) that Yeshua compared Yohanan, his one-time rabbi, with Elijah. The
comparison is now extended to himself and Elisha, and
it is especially apt, for two reasons. First, Elisha claimed
an endowment with the spirit greater than his teacher's,
and that is also involved in the story of Yeshua's immersion by Yohanan (as described in chapter 2). Second,
Elisha's endowment with the spirit is sealed by a vision,
of Elijah's ascent, and that is comparable to Yeshua's vision of the spirit (again, discussed at some length in
chapter 2). The fragment from Qumran, which was

our point of departure in this section, helps us to see the messianic associations of the spirit which featured especially in Yeshua's characterization of his own activity.

The fragment is also instructive of how Yeshua saw the spirit in relation to the kingdom of God. "Over the meek his spirit will hover," the fragment states, and "he will glorify the pious ones on the throne of the eternal kingdom." The proximity of the spirit marks the effective presence of God's kingdom. That kingdom, of course, was the central theme in the theology of Yeshua, and he specifically linked the kingdom with his own endowment with the spirit. The dynamic quality of transcendence in Yeshua's teaching is evident in a famous saying from "Q" (Matt. 12:28; Luke 11:20):

> If I by the spirit of God cast out demons,
> then the kingdom of God has arrived upon you.

Because Yeshua's own activity is the particular occasion of the kingdom here ("If I by the spirit of God . . . "), an implicit christology is involved. The unspoken assertion is that his exorcisms are effective of the kingdom in a way that others' are not,[11] and the reference to the spirit explains why that is the case.

Mention has already been made (p. 54) of the reversal of fortunes which the book of Haggai depicts on the basis of the activity of God's spirit. God is portrayed

---

11. For further discussion, see Bruce Chilton, *Pure Kingdom: Jesus' Vision of God,* Studying the Historical Jesus 1 (Eerdmans: Grand Rapids, 1996), 67–70.

as stirring the spirit of Zerubbabel, the Davidic king, and Joshua, the high priest, and all the people through Haggai (see Hag. 1:14). God's spirit in the midst of Israel (Hag. 2:5) permits of the restoration of the Temple, so that blessing is again possible (Hag. 2:19). That is the foundation of the prediction of the purification of worship in the Temple in Zechariah (see Zech. 4:6 for another key reference to God's spirit) and the prediction of the coming of Elijah in Malachi. All of that explains why Yeshua would eventually have pointed his teaching toward the Temple, the place where purity and holiness were to be manifest for all Israel. But the teaching which was worked out in the Temple, and produced his final confrontation with the authorities there, was actually developed in Galilee. That was where the restoration of purity and consequent healing were paired within the practice and theology of Yeshua, as we have repeatedly seen.

The Galilean Program of Purity

In Galilee (as we saw in chapter 2), Yeshua began to announce the kingdom of God as drawing near and stopped immersing people as a characteristic activity. He distinguished himself clearly from Yohanan precisely by elevating his former teacher to the status of Elijah. The meal replaced immersion as the principal symbolic activity, and the focus became the fact of purity which God's kingdom sanctified by its presence rather than the achievement of purity. Healing — in the cases of cleansing the man with "outbreak," curing the woman with a hemorrhage, and raising Yair's daughter — consistently involves redrawing the lines of purity. "Outbreak," blood, and death are included within the restored life of Israel in these instances because Yeshua, the physician of contagious purity, extends to them the benefits of cleanness.

Contemporary research, including archaeological discoveries, has greatly enhanced our understanding of the cultural complexion of Galilee. As Richard Horsley has explained, until the most recent study, there has been a tendency over the past decade to exaggerate the integration of Galilee within the Graeco-Roman world. Because the cities of Sepphoris and Tiberias, both substantial sites, had been excavated, the supposition was that they represented Galilean culture as such. The problem is first that both cities were not of the importance or influence of Ptolemais, Scythopolis, Caesarea Maritima, and Jerusalem, all of which were outside Galilee.[12] Second, neither city could be said to have deserved the loyalty of those who lived around them. Sepphoris was essentially a fortress town for Herod and Herod Antipas. When Herod himself died, Judas (the son of an outlaw whom Herod had killed) led a group on a raid of the royal fortress (see Josephus, *Antiquities* 17 §§271–

---

12. See Richard A. Horsley, *Archaeology, History, and Society in Galilee: The Social Context of Jesus and the Rabbis* (Valley Forge, Pa.: Trinity Press International, 1996), 43–47.

72). It was then up to the Roman legate Varus to retake
Sepphoris and punish the populace (so *Antiquities* 17
§289), and up to Herod Antipas later to repair and even
enhance the city (so *Antiquities* 18 §27), renaming it
"Imperial City." Not even Herod Antipas showed much
faith in the future of Sepphoris as the seat of his power.
In 18 c.e., he founded Tiberias (named after the emperor) on the Sea of Galilee,[13] on a site which included
a disused cemetery. Josephus goes out of his way to em-
phasize the poor background of the Galileans who were
encouraged and even compelled to settle there, among
whom some were involved in the collection of taxes (see
Antiquities 18 §§36–38).

The consequences of recognizing these realities are
quite dramatic for an understanding of the context of
earliest Christianity, as Horsley goes on to say:

> To say that the culture was already urban as well as
> rural and therefore prepared for Roman dominance
> is untrue both of Galilee and of Judea proper. In
> fact, such a generalization flies in the face of the
> history of Palestine during what archaeologists call
> the "Early Roman" period (Pompey through Bar
> Kokhba). In late second-temple Judea proper the
> only city was Jerusalem itself. Prior to Antipas,
> with only the administrative town of Sepphoris
> (the size of which at that time is still unclear), Gal-
> ilee was hardly urbanized. The popular rebellions

---

13. See ibid., 49–51.

against the Roman conquerors and/or their client-rulers in 40–37 B.C.E., 4 B.C.E., and 66–70 C.E., as well as several ad hoc protests and resistance movements among both Judeans and Galileans in the Early Roman period, hardly indicate a people prepared for Roman domination and favorable to urbanization.[14]

Resistance to the Roman city is much more characteristic among the Galileans than an acceptance of Graeco-Roman urbanization, and urbanization of Galilee in any case became a Roman policy only during the second century, after the revolt of Simeon bar Kosiba (132–35 C.E.).[15]

The Galilee in which Yeshua announced the kingdom of God and healed, and sent out delegates with the same program, was a region of small villages:

The vast majority of Galileans were thus members of a village community. Villages consisted of a smaller or larger number of families or households. As the most fundamental social form in a traditional agrarian society, the household was the

---

14. Ibid., 54–55. He also rightly observes that the hypothesis of Jesus as a Cynic philosopher, an attempt to "de-Judaize Jesus and place him into a more cosmopolitan cultural context" (1), is simply ruled out by a consideration of the archaeological and historical sources (179–85).

15. See Lee I. Levine, *The Rabbinic Class of Palestine in Late Antiquity* (New York: Jewish Theological Seminary of America, 1989).

basic unit of production and consumption. According to the Israelite ideal (similar to that of other peasantries), each family worked and lived from the produce of its ancestral inheritance of land. Each household produced most of what it consumed and consumed much of what it produced. As indicated by both rabbinic texts and archaeological excavations, within the village settlement each family lived in a "house" of a small room or two (3m x 4m) opening off of a courtyard shared with one or more other families. In the courtyard they shared use of oven, millstone, and cistern. In the village they shared use of a common wine-press and olive-press.... The majority of settlements, occupying from two to five acres with roughly 40 to 60 people per acre, would have included fewer than 300 people each.[16]

Horsley accepts Josephus's count that there were "204 cities and villages in Galilee" (*Life* §235), and he describes the characteristic ethos (in a major heading in a chapter) as "active opposition to the cities."[17]

Yeshua returned to this Galilee, away from the relatively sparse Peraea[18] and its association with Herod Antipas's deadly reassertion of his power by means of

---

16. Horsley, *Archaeology, History, and Society in Galilee*, 89.

17. Ibid., 123.

18. The only region of Israel described by Josephus as wilderness, although he also refers to fertile portions (*War* 3 §§44–47). By contrast, he says that Galilee is well cultivated (*War* §§41–43), and that

killing Yohanan. Horsley develops a model of what he calls the regionalism of Galilee, which represents a major advance in understanding. He refutes the attempt to characterize Lower Galilee as urban and Upper Galilee as rural during the time of Yeshua and argues that the more basic cultural differences throughout Galilee "were probably between the cities and the villages, not between Upper Galilean villages and Lower Galilean villages."[19] But aside from some resistance to urban, Roman culture, what was the ethos of these villages? Horsley suggests some "separate development" of "Israelite traditions such as the Mosaic covenant," which he calls a "'little tradition' or popular customs," in contrast to the "'great tradition' of the Jerusalem temple-state."[20]

That characterization is basic to Horsley's take on Galilean regionalism, and it must be refined in order to understand Yeshua's activity, even as the real strengths of this scheme should be acknowledged. Here we find a thematic emphasis that Aramaic was the language of the Galileans,[21] that the "oral 'little' tradition of the traditional village life" would likely have recalled the stories of Saul, David, Jeroboam, and Jehu, as well as

---

Judaea and Samaria are rich in wild and cultivated plants (*War* 3 §§48–50).

19. Horsley, *Archaeology, History, and Society in Galilee*, 93; see the discussion as a whole on pp. 88–95 .

20. Ibid., 95; see also p. 122.

21. Ibid., 106, 154–71, 177. On the last page cited, he acknowledges that his mind has changed in this regard.

Mount Tabor and — above all — Elijah,[22] that the synagogue in first-century Galilee was not a building but a congregation for the purpose of guiding the community.[23] All that has been argued on the basis of literary sources alone, especially viewed from the angle of cultural anthropology,[24] but Horsley provides a much-needed collation with archaeological evidence. That work needs to go on, and particular attention should be paid to what James F. Strange has recently referred to:

A unique item in the material culture of the Early Roman Jewish world was a class of soft, white stone vessels which appear in no less than sixty-five sites all over ancient Palestine. At least fourteen of these sites are in Upper and Lower Galilee (Gush Halav, Nabratein, Meiron, Kefar Hana-

---

22. Ibid., 112, 171–75.

23. Ibid., 145–53. This section is especially interesting for its reference to the Mishnah in order to characterize synagogues in Galilee. But Horsley's assumption that communal regulation of this sort was "democratic" needs to be tested against both historical and ethnographic evidence. See also Kenneth Atkinson, "On Further Defining the First-Century C.E. Synagogue: Fact or Fiction?" *New Testament Studies* 43, no. 4 (1997): 491–502.

24. Indeed, I am struck with the overlap with Chilton, *A Galilean Rabbi and His Bible: Jesus' Use of the Interpreted Scripture of His Time* (Wilmington: Glazier, 1984), also published with the subtitle *Jesus' Own Interpretation of Isaiah* (London: SPCK, 1984), and Bruce Chilton, *The Temple of Jesus: His Sacrificial Program within a Cultural History of Sacrifice* (University Park: Pennsylvania State University Press, 1992).

niah, Capernaum, Yodfat, Jotapata, Ibelin, Kefar Kenna, Sepphoris, Reina, Nazareth, Bethlehem of Galilee, Migdal Ha-Emeq, and Tiberias).... These vessels were evidently designed to meet the requirements of laws of purity. They seem to be distinctively Jewish, as they only superficially resemble the marble vessels well known in the Roman world.[25]

Evidently, purity is a category of analysis which the mounting archaeological evidence demands, and which Horsley all but ignores.

Moreover, there is a range of material which Horsley ignores entirely, material stemming from the very source which he principally uses to characterize the Galileans: Josephus's writings. He is right, of course, to point out the lack of reference by many modern scholars to the facts surrounding the sack of Sepphoris by some Galileans (*War* 2 §56; *Antiquities* 17 §§271–72);[26] such passages are an important support for his particular version of Galilean regionalism. But there is an another range of passages, implicating the Galileans in violence, which demand a further refinement of how that regionalism is to be understood. Time and again, over a period of more than a century, Josephus associates Galileans with violence in the Temple in Jerusalem.

---

25. James F. Strange, "First-Century Galilee from Archaeology and from the Texts," in Edwards and McCollough, eds., *Archaeology and the Galilee,* 39–48, 44.

26. Richard Horsley, in Edwards and McCollough, eds., *Archaeology and the Galilee,* 111–12.

In the aftermath of the death of Herod the Great, Josephus describes the rebellions which broke out in some detail. At Pentecost, crowds gathered at the Temple from Galilee and elsewhere, not for worship alone, but in order to confront the Roman procurator. They made the Temple the center of a military assault on the Romans, in the course of which the Romans set fire to the outer porticos of the Temple and then engaged in looting (*Antiquities* 17 §§254–64). That by no means put an end to such rebellion, which continued in Jerusalem and throughout Judaea (*Antiquities* 17 §§265–70), and it is *in this context* that Josephus goes on to speak of the sack of Sepphoris by Judas the son of Hezekiah. What is at issue here is not a coordinated campaign by a single strategist, but something far more evocative: an outburst of Galilean fervor which was centered on the Temple and which expressed itself in overt violence toward the Romans.

The damage which occurred in 4 B.C.E. was light compared to the extensive destruction involved in 37 B.C.E., when Herod the Great and the Romans besieged Jerusalem and the Temple (see *Antiquities* 14 §§465–91). The end of that siege marked the close of Hasmonean rule and permitted Herod's significant redesign of the Temple (see *Antiquities* 15 §§380–425). It is not surprising that Herod had to deal with significant resistance in Galilee. Josephus describes him as taking some of Antigonus's strongholds there, including Sepphoris, but then had to contend with "thugs [*lestai*] dwelling in caves" near Arbela (*Antiquities* 14

§§413–17). In other words, Herod had to contend with a disorganized Galilean resistance, as well as with Antigonus and his Parthian backing. It is no wonder that Josephus mentions Galilean rebellion subsequently, and Herod's bloody response (for example, *Antiquities* 14 §§431–33). When Josephus speaks of the "people as a whole" gathered in Jerusalem to resist Herod (so *Antiquities* 14 §470), it is evident that Galileans were included.

The dreadful events of 37 B.C.E. and 4 B.C.E. were followed by the more thorough (and better known) destruction of the Temple in 70 C.E. What is frequently not remarked, however, is that a key player in the resistance to the Romans *in Jerusalem as well as in Galilee* was Josephus's great rival, known usually as John of Gischala (after Josephus's Greek text). "Gischala" is none other than Gush Halav, one of the villages in Galilee which has recently been excavated.[27] Galilean resistance to Rome focused naturally on the Temple in Jerusalem, which Galileans appropriated as their own symbol.

Horsley does not attend to the evidence of this pattern because his view of regionalism is excessively territorial. He writes, "There can be no question of any effective integration of the Galileans into the Judean temple-community."[28] Although his attempt to discover characteristic features of Galilean Judaism is seminal, the belief that it can simply be divorced from the Ju-

---

27. See ibid., 96–101.
28. Ibid., 28; see also 11, 182.

daism of the Temple is naive. Certainly, that was not
the conviction of some Galileans who, during their pil-
grimage to Jerusalem for a festival, were attacked by
Samaritans. When the leading people of the Galileans
sought relief from Cumanus, the Roman governor, he
refused them; the result was the sack of Samaritan villages led by Eleazar, son of Deinaeus, whom Josephus
describes as a "thug" who made his way of life in the
mountains (*Antiquities* 20 §§118–24). It was this increase of what Josephus calls "thuggery" which marks
the mounting violence, from around the year 63 c.e.,
which climaxed in the burning of the Temple under Ti-
tus. The link between Galilee, violence, and the Temple
could not be plainer. The laconic reference in Luke 13:1
to Pilate's mingling of the blood of some Galileans with
their sacrifices is gruesome, but in character both with
the Galileans and Pilate.[29]

In his extended criticism of John of Gischala, Josephus also elucidates (quite inadvertently) the religious
perspective of one Galilean militant. Josephus criticizes
his rival in Galilee for an arrangement in which Jews in

---

29. See C. F. D. Moule, "Some Observations on *Tendenzkritik*,"
in *Jesus and the Politics of His Day,* ed. E. Bammel and C. F. D.
Moule (Cambridge: Cambridge University Press, 1984), 91–100, 95–
96. The Galilean pattern of violence in the Temple renders attempts
to associate Luke 13:1 with what happened under Cumanus (or earlier, in 4 b.c.e.) superfluous. The pattern was so strong, it seems
obvious that there were many incidents of which there is no record.
Josephus does not mention Yeshua's occupation of the Temple, for
example, although Mark indicates it was associated with a riot (see
Mark 15:7).

Syria would purchase oil from a Galilean source (*War 2* §§591–92; *Life* §§73–74).[30] The criticism is that John was motivated by the desire for profit, but the concern for purity — on the assumption that Galilean oil was pure — is manifest in both the vendors and the purchasers. As Horsley points out, in his description of Galilee "Josephus even draws a connection between the rural, agricultural character of Galilee and the people's passion for independence of outside rulers."[31] That John of Gischala's program extended from the provision of Galilean oil to the siege in Jerusalem shows that Galilean "regionalism" was in no sense limited to the territory of Galilee. Rather, the products of Galilee were themselves part of that purity of Israel which was to be established in the Temple, as well.

A final example from the pages of Josephus may further help to orient us for an understanding of a Galilean construction of purity. In his description of the conversion of King Izates, son of Helena of Adiabene, Josephus names one Eleazar from Galilee[32] as requiring the king to be circumcised, against contrary advice (*Antiquities* 20 §§43–48). The principle of his advice is that the laws are not only to be read, but performed, so that it would be an offense against the law of Moses to

---

30. See Chilton, *The Temple of Jesus*, 75; Horsley, in Edwards and McCollough, eds., *Archaeology and the Galilee*, 68–69.

31. Horsley, in Edwards and McCollough, eds., *Archaeology and the Galilee*, 88, citing *War* 3 §§41–44.

32. It is noteworthy that Eleazar is styled as "strict" (*akribes*); various forms of that word are applied to Pharisees in Acts 22:3; 26:5.

claim to maintain the traditions of Judaism, and yet not to be circumcised. Although Eleazar may not be claimed as an example of Galilean Judaism as a whole, what he does instance is how a Galilean could turn his enthusiasm for one practice of the religion into a requirement basic to the whole of the Torah. Yeshua's adherence to Yohanan's movement of immersion is another example, as is his famous citation of the twin commandments, to love God and neighbor, as the greatest (Matt. 23:34–40; Mark 12:28–34; compare Luke 10:25–28).

Of course, Yeshua's shift from being an immerser to announcing the kingdom signaled the change of theology (and of eschatology) we considered in the last chapter. But directly associated with that change, and far more immediately obvious to observers, was Yeshua's radical change in the understanding of the medium and the means of purity. Where Yohanan had insisted upon repentance and water as the way to purification by immersion, Yeshua stressed forgiveness and contact as the way to purification by communal eating. Yeshua's practice of contagious purity claimed for himself what John of Gischala claimed for the oil of his own village.

Yeshua's conviction that the spirit of God was active within him has already been explained, particularly in relation to the book of Haggai. To that reference we may add the clear statement in the book of Zechariah, made to Zerubbabel of the house of David, that he would found the Temple by means of God's own spirit, and by no other means (see Zech. 4:6). That connection, of course, is highly significant, because Zechariah 14 provided Yeshua with the prophetic precedent to empty the courts of the Temple of the vendors he found there.[33]

But Zechariah provides insight into the coherence of Yeshua's actions, not only in Jerusalem, but also in Galilee, and even Samaria. In Zechariah 13:1 the prophet promises:

> In that day there shall be a fountain opened for the house of David and the inhabitants of Jerusalem in view of sin and uncleanness.

That image, in turn, relates to the "living waters" which are to flow from Jerusalem as the center of all the nations (14:8).[34] "Living waters," in the form of "a fountain of living waters springing up to eternal life," is what Yeshua promises the Samaritan woman in the Gospel according to John (4:14). In a different key, that is a statement of the sort of purification Yeshua extends to the man with "outbreak," the woman with a flow of blood, and Yair's daughter. Provided with God's spirit, Yeshua claims to be a son of David who conveys purity.

Yeshua's Davidic role in conveying the health which comes of purity is especially stressed in those passages where he is addressed as "son of David." Recent scholarship has proven that the phrase might be applied to a person as a healer, one gifted in the way that Solomon,

---

33. See Chilton, *Jesus' Prayer and Jesus' Eucharist.*

34. For additional connections between Yeshua's program and Zechariah, see Chilton, *The Temple of Jesus,* 135–36.

David's first son, was.[35] Indeed, Solomon's ability, according to one text from Qumran, derived rather directly from his father, since David had composed songs "for making music over the stricken" (11QPSa Dav Comp).[36] Yeshua, it turns out, is chiefly called "David's son" within the contexts of his healing (see Matt. 9:27–31; 20:29–34; Mark 10:46–52; Luke 18:35–43). Within the Synoptic Gospels, that is the predominant context of the reference, although Matthew develops a particularly genealogical interest in the descent of the Messiah.[37]

In fact, a single story effects this focus on healing and the son of David:

[46]And they come into Jericho. And when he and his students came out of Jericho with a sizable

---

35. See Loren R. Fisher, "Can This Be the Son of David?" *Jesus and the Historian: Written in Honour of Ernest Cadman Colwell,* ed. F. T. Trotter (Philadelphia: Westminster, 1968), 82–97; D. C. Duling, "Solomon, Exorcism, and the Son of David," *Harvard Theological Review* 68 (1975): 235–52; S. Giverson, "Solomon und die Dämonen," *Essays on the Nag Hammadi Texts in Honour of Alexander Böhlig,* Nag Hammadi Studies 3, ed. M. Krause (Leiden: Brill, 1972), 16–21.

36. See J. A. Sanders, *The Psalm Scroll of Qumran Cave 11,* Discoveries in the Judaean Desert of Jordan 4 (Oxford: Clarendon, 1965), 92. There is a dispute in the scholarly literature whether "son of David" should be taken as a title which is applied to Yeshua. (Fisher and Duling represent the dispute lucidly.) Whether it is or not, there can be little question that the phrase was associated with healing, and that Yeshua was, too.

37. See Chilton, "Jesus *ben David:* Reflections on the *Davidssohnfrage,*" *Journal for the Study of the New Testament* 14 (1982): 88–112.

crowd, Bartimayah — the son of Timayah, a blind beggar — was sitting by the way. [47] He heard that it was Yeshua Nazarene and began to shout out and say,

David's son, Yeshua, have mercy on me.

[48] And many scolded him so that he would be silent, but he rather shouted all the more,

David's son, have mercy on me.

[49] Yeshua stood still and said, Call him. They call the blind man and say to him, Courage, arise, he calls you. [50] But he threw aside his garment, jumped up, and came to Yeshua. [51] Yeshua responded to him and said,

What do you want me to do?

But the blind man said to him,

Rabbouni, so I might see again.

[52] And Yeshua said to him,

Go away, your faith has saved you.

And at once he saw again and followed him on the way. (Mark 10:46–52)

The basis on which Yeshua acts here is clearly set out in what Bar Timayah says: as David's son and rabbi, Yeshua is in a position to heal the blind man and to declare him pure in a single breath.

The story takes up elements of passages which appear earlier in Mark and provides them with a single focus. Immediately before Peter's confession of Yeshua as Messiah (a confession whose implication of triumph without suffering Yeshua rejects; Mark 8:27–33), Mark presents the story of a healing of a blind man at Bethsaida in Galilee (Mark 8:22–26). It portrays Yeshua as engaging in quasi-magical manipulations: he takes the man by the hand out of the village, spits into his eyes, and touches him twice prior to the full healing.[38] Similar procedures, complete with the Aramaic term *Ephphatha*, which Yeshua used in the healing, are related in the story of the deaf mute (7:31–37). Neither of those healings finds its way into Luke or Matthew; the degree of manipulative action on Yeshua's part must have seemed strange to those who portrayed Yeshua as healing by a mere word (see Matt. 8:5–13; Luke 7:1–10).[39] But both stories reflect the Solomonic conception of a son of David who heals by means of the wisdom of his predecessors: what Bar Timayah has to say specifies that conception.

Similarly, Bar Timayah's specification that Yeshua acts as a rabbi here serves as a resumé of the many in-

---

38. See Morton Smith, *Jesus the Magician* (San Francisco: Harper, 1981).

39. That vignette concerns more the scope of Yeshua's program of healing than the details of how he healed. Nonetheless, the similarity with a story concerning Rabbi Ḥanina ben Dosa is striking; see Berakhoth 34b and the discussion in George Foot Moore, *Judaism in the First Centuries of the Christian Era* (Cambridge: Harvard University Press, 1962), 236.

stances in Mark in which Yeshua has behaved as a rabbi: teaching in synagogues (Mark 1:21–22), cleansing the man with "outbreak" (1:40–45), declaring forgiveness and healing on that basis (2:1–12), establishing a circle of fellowship at meals (2:15–18) as well as principles of fasting (2:18–22) and keeping Sabbath (2:23–28), healing in synagogue (3:1–5), and setting out a system of purity (chapter 7). When Bar Timayah calls Yeshua both "David's son" and "Rabbi," he associates healing and purification in a way which identifies what has been going on in the narrative from the beginning. Bar Timayah's statement also permits us to see that when Yeshua's action is more a matter of purification (as "rabbi"), his healing is by means of a verbal declaration; when his action is more a matter of cure (as "David's son"), his healing is more a matter of manipulation and contact.

In the story of the healing of Bar Timayah, Yeshua is portrayed as accepting the designations "David's son" and "rabbi" in the precise applications of healing and purification. That he does so is especially poignant in view of what follows. Entering into Jerusalem, the crowds shout out, "Blessed be the coming kingdom of our father, David!" (Mark 11:10). That is to say, they take Yeshua's Davidic descent, together with his preaching and his actions, to signal his messianic status. They make the same mistake Peter did in his confession at Caesarea Philippi. The crowd's expectation is not a surprise, in view of the royal treatment given the descendant of David in *Psalms of Solomon* 17, a work from the first century B.C.E.

Indeed his position was pointed against such teaching when Yeshua asked, "How do the scribes say that the Messiah is David's son?" (Mark 12:35). The sense of that rhetorical question is that Yeshua, descended from the house of David, was not for that reason putting himself up as a royal Messiah.[40] What he does in the Temple is an extension of his Galilean perspective on purity: his conviction that Israel was to offer of Israel's own, not the objects of trade on the site. His purifications and his healings were part of the same program of suiting Israel for the offering of worship with the integrity demanded by God.

Davidic descent could be used by Yeshua, as it was by other rabbis,[41] to authorize his position. That, indeed, might explain why the phrase "son of David" is directed toward Yeshua in the context of healing in the vicinity of Jerusalem, rather than in Galilee. But the authority Yeshua appealed to characteristically, as we have seen, was the spirit of God:

> If I by the spirit of God put out demons, then the
> kingdom of God has come upon you. (Matt. 12:28)

The entire issue of demons, of course, is related to the question of healing, but exorcisms should be dealt with

---

40. That is the point of the exegesis developed in Chilton, "Jesus *ben David*."

41. The examples of Hillel, Judah the prince, Ḥiyya, and Ḥuna are cited in Jacob Neusner, *A History of the Jews in Babylonia* 1, Studia Post-Biblica 9 (Leiden: Brill, 1965), 35f., 101–4, 175–76. See also the works cited in Chilton, "Jesus *ben David*," 110–11, n. 47.

separately. They are more akin to the signs of Yeshua, such as his feeding of multitudes, than to the healings and purifications of Yeshua. Where a sign is directed to the understanding, healings and purifications directly restore people to the body of Israel and therefore — in Yeshua's thinking — to the solidarity of the Temple. But the source of his healings/purifications is the same as the source of his exorcisms: the spirit released during his immersion by Yohanan provided Yeshua with insight and vision, and also with the power to purify and heal. The same book of Zechariah which has provided vital clues to Yeshua's program of purity and his occupation of the Temple also speaks of God's spirit being set in the north country of Israel (see Zech. 6:8). In the case of Yeshua, that reference finds a particular enactment.

≈ 4 ≈

Baptism into the Name of Jesus

At the level of theology and at the level of practice, the development of the movement Yeshua began into Christianity is punctuated by two drastic changes. The first change (as we saw in chapter 2) is when Yeshua himself stopped immersing people after the example of Yohanan, his own rabbi. The reasons for and the implications of that change have been explored in the chapters which precede. The second change is proportionate to and symmetrical with the first: after Yeshua was experienced as risen from the dead, his disciples began to immerse people in dedication to him (as they said in Greek, "into the name of Jesus"). Baptism in that sense has seemed so obvious a ritual within Christianity, the question has never been posed: why did Yeshua's disciples begin to do in his name precisely what he personally did *not* do as part of his characteristic activity?

In a recent study of baptism in the New Testament, Lars Hartman has observed that the phrase "into the name of" is not idiomatic Greek, but more probably reflects the Aramaic *leshun* (or Hebrew *leshem*). He adduces a passage from the Mishnah (Zebahim 4:6) in order to explain the meaning of the phrase.[1] There, the phrase clearly refers to those "for the sake of" whom a given sacrifice is offered.[2] Having understood that the generative meaning of the phrase is cultic, Hartman explains the significance of baptism in terms of the new community which is called into being:

> Here the people of the new covenant were gathered, cleansed, forgiven, sanctified and equipped with a new spirit. Indeed, the gathering itself can also be regarded as occurring "into the name of the Lord Jesus."[3]

Such an emphasis on the role of God's spirit in baptism is fundamental from the point of view of the New Testament itself, as we shall see. Whether the formulation is of immersion "into" or "in" Jesus' name, the latter simply being better Greek, in either case the point is that Jesus is the occasion and place where the spirit is encountered. Still, Hartman's study leaves open the question of why a phrase of cultic origin should have been used in connection with baptism. That is an issue which we shall

---

1. Lars Hartman, *"Into the Name of the Lord Jesus": Baptism in the Early Church*, Studies of the New Testament and Its World (Edinburgh: Clark, 1997), 37–50.

2. That is precisely the translation in Jacob Neusner, *The Mishnah: A New Translation* (New Haven: Yale University Press, 1988), 707. See also Pesahim 60a, cited by Hartman, *"Into the Name of the Lord,"* 49 n. 53.

3. Hartman, *"Into the Name of the Lord Jesus,"* 47.

also address as we observe the emergence of a new significance of Yohanan's and Yeshua's immersion after the resurrection.

In his resumé of the usual presentation of Christian baptism in the New Testament, G. B. Caird observes the close connection between immersion and the gift of the spirit of God:

> The case of Cornelius, in which the Spirit came first and baptism followed (Acts 10:47f.), was an exception to the normal pattern (Acts 2:38) that the Spirit followed baptism.[4]

Those two cases, in Cornelius's house and in Jerusalem at Pentecost, do in fact embrace the overall model of baptism as presented within the book of Acts, the principal source for the practice within the earliest church. The first instance Caird mentions, the baptisms authorized by Peter in the house of the Roman officer Cornelius (Acts 10), represents the principle of the Petrine extension of activity far outside Jerusalem.[5] The other reference is the famous scene of the mass baptisms (of some three thousand people, according to Acts 2:41) following the events at Pentecost.

---

4. G. B. Caird, *New Testament Theology*, ed. L. D. Hurst (Oxford: Clarendon, 1994), 224.

5. For a discussion of the extension and its theological underpinnings, see Jacob Neusner and Bruce D. Chilton, *The Body of Faith: Israel and the Church*, Christianity and Judaism — The Formative Categories (Valley Forge, Pa.: Trinity Press International, 1996), 129–33.

But before the contrast between those two scenes can be assessed, the underlying unity of their account of what baptism into Yeshua's name involves needs to be appreciated. In each case, the principal agent of baptism, and the person who provides the theology to account for the practice and the attendant experience, is Peter. And the theological account he provides is quite coherent as one moves in order from Acts 2 to Acts 10.

Baptism in the Circle of Peter

At Pentecost, the spirit is portrayed as descending on the twelve apostles (including the newly chosen Matthiyah), and they speak God's praises in the various languages of those assembled from the four points of the compass for that summer feast of harvest, both Jews and proselytes (Acts 2:1–12). The mention of proselytes (2:10) and the stress that those gathered came from "every nation under heaven" (2:5) clearly point ahead to the inclusion of non-Jews by means of baptism within Acts.[6] But even Peter's explanation of the descent of the spirit does that. He quotes from the prophet Joel (3:1–5 in the Septuagint),

---

6. So C. K. Barrett, *The Acts of the Apostles* 1, International Critical Commentary (Edinburgh: Clark, 1994), 108. See also Hartman, *"Into the Name of the Lord Jesus,"* 131–33, who observes the coherence with Luke 24:44–49. That is a telling remark, because it shows, together with the preaching attributed to Peter in the house of Cornelius, that the narrative of Yeshua's passion was connected with the catechesis which led to baptism from a primitive stage.

"And it will be in the last days, says God, that I will pour out from my spirit upon all flesh."[7] "All flesh," not only historic Israel, is to receive of God's spirit.

Pentecost is the most notable feast (in calendrical terms) of Peter and his circle. Seven weeks after the close of the entire festival of Passover and Unleavened Bread came the feast called Weeks or Pentecost (in Greek, referring to the period of fifty days that was involved; see Lev. 23:15–22; Deut. 16:9–12). The waving of the sheaf before the LORD at the close of Passover anticipated the greater harvest (especially of wheat; see Exod. 34:22) which was to follow in the summer, and that is just what Weeks celebrates (so Lev. 23:10–15). The timing of the coming of the holy spirit in the recollection of Peter's circle is unequivocal (Acts 2:1–4), and the theme of Moses dispensing the spirit on his elders is reflected (see Num. 11:11–29). The association of Weeks with the covenant with Noah (see *Jubilees* 6:1, 10–11, 17–19) may help to explain why the coming of spirit then was to extend to humanity at large (see Acts 2:5–11). First fruits were celebrated at Weeks (see Num. 28:26) and they are used to express the gift of spirit and resurrection in Paul's theology (Rom. 8:23; 11:16; 1 Cor. 15:20, 23). We should expect such connections with the Pentecostal theology of Peter in one of Peter's students (see Gal. 1:18), as we should expect him to be especially concerned to keep the feast of Pentecost (see 1 Cor. 16:8; Acts 20:16)

---

7. Ibid., 129–57, presents a fine analysis on how deeply influential the text of Joel is on the speech of Peter as a whole.

despite what he said about calendrical observations in Galatians (see Gal. 4:9–10; cf. 2:14).

Now we are in a position to see why it was natural within the Petrine circle to speak of immersion "into the name of Jesus": the cultic language was inspired by the environment of Pentecost. Those who entered into a fresh relationship to God by means of the holy spirit were themselves a kind of "first fruits," finding their identity in relation to Christ or spirit as "first fruit" (so Rom. 8:23; 11:16; 16:5; 1 Cor. 15:20, 23; 16:15; James 1:18; Rev. 14:4). The wide range of that usage, which attests to the influence of the Petrine theology (see the next section), reflects the deeply Pentecostal character of primitive Christianity. Access to the covenant by means of the spirit meant that they entered sacrificially "into the name" (*eis to onoma*) of Jesus in baptism. Also within the Petrine circle, Eucharist was celebrated in covenantal terms, when one broke bread and shared the cup "into the remembrance of" (*eis ten anamnesin*) of Jesus, a phrase associated with covenantal sacrifice.[8] Both baptism and Eucharist are sacrificial in the Petrine understanding, and both intimately involve the spirit of God.

Hartman makes a similar point in regard to the continuing presence of spirit in his discussion of a famous passage for Paul:

---

8. See Chilton, *Jesus' Prayer and Jesus' Eucharist.* Hartman, *"Into the Name of the Lord Jesus,"* 61, also approaches this idea.

> For just as the body is one and has many members, but all the members of the body, being many, are one body, so is Christ. Because by one spirit we were all immersed into one body, whether Jews or Greeks, whether slaves or free, and we were all made to drink one spirit. (1 Cor. 12:12–13)

As Hartman observes:

> The last clause of the verse, "We were all made to drink of one Spirit," could as well be translated "We all had the one Spirit poured over us." The Spirit not only brought the baptized persons into the body of Christ, but also remains with them as a divine active presence.[9]

Spirit is understood to be the continuing medium of faithful existence in Christ, and for that reason it is as natural to associate it with Eucharist as with baptism. After all, Paul could also say that believers, like the Israelites, drank the same spiritual drink, which came from Christ (1 Cor. 10:4[10]), and that the Israelites went through their own immersion (1 Cor. 10:2).

When Peter is speaking in the house of Cornelius in Acts 10, the spirit falls upon those who are listening, and those there with Peter who were circumcised were astounded "that the gift of the holy spirit has been poured even upon the nations" (10:44–45). The choice

---

9. Hartman, *"Into the Name of the Lord Jesus,"* 67–68.

10. Paul's insistence here that the rock was Christ might be intended to qualify the claims of the Petrine circle.

of the verb "to pour" is no coincidence: it is resonant with the quotation of Joel in Acts 2:17. Indeed, those in Cornelius's house praise God "in tongues" (10:46)[11] in a manner reminiscent of the apostles' prophecy at Pentecost, and Peter directs that they be baptized "in the name of Christ Jesus" (10:47–48). That is just the direction Peter gave earlier to his sympathetic hearers at Pentecost (2:37–38). Probably in the case of his speech at Pentecost, and more definitely in the case of his speech in the house of Cornelius, Peter's directions were in Greek, and we should understand that immersion is not in any general sense and that "Jesus" (*Iesous*) has entered the Greek language as the preferred name for Yeshua. Christian baptism, immersion into the name of Jesus with reception of the holy spirit, was developed within the practice of the circle of Peter.

In aggregate, the two passages do not suggest any real dispute as to whether the gift of the spirit followed or preceded baptism into Jesus' name. The point is rather that belief in and baptism into him is connected directly with the outpouring of God's spirit. The apparent disruption of the usual model in Acts 10 is intended to call attention to the artificiality (from the point of view of the emergent Petrine theology) of attempting to withhold baptism from those who believe (as Peter actually

---

11. The assumption here and in Acts 2 is that spirit makes people more articulate than they normally are. That is also the way Paul believes tongues are properly to be conceived, as opposed to those who see the gift of tongues as resulting in incoherence (see 1 Cor. 14).

says in 10:47).[12] Two questions immediately arise at this point. First, why would it have been so natural for Peter to have extended baptism to non-Jews on the basis of the outpouring of spirit, when he was still sensitive to the scruples of Judaism? (And that sensitivity is recorded by Paul, a contemporary witness; see Gal. 2:11–14.[13]) Second, where did Peter understand the new infusion of spirit to have derived from?

As it happens, those two questions have a single answer. The source of the spirit is Jesus as raised from the dead. In Peter's speech at Pentecost, Jesus, having been exalted to the right hand of God, receives the promise of the holy spirit from the father and pours it out on his followers (2:33). The spirit which is poured out, then, comes directly from the majesty of God, from his rule over creation as a whole. This is the spirit as it hovered over the waters at the beginning of creation (Gen. 1:2), and not as limited to Israel. Because the spirit is of God, who creates people in the divine image, its presence marks God's own activity, in which all those who follow Jesus are to be included. Jesus' own program had involved proclaiming God's kingdom on the authority of his possession of God's spirit (see above, pp. 45–55). Now, as a consequence of the resurrection, Jesus had poured out that same spirit upon those who would follow him. Baptism in the spirit (see Acts 1:4–5) and baptism into the

---

12. See Hartman, *"Into the Name of the Lord Jesus,"* 133–36.

13. For a discussion, see Bruce Chilton and Jacob Neusner, *Judaism in the New Testament: Practices and Beliefs* (London: Routledge, 1995), 99–104, 108–11.

name of Jesus were one and the same thing for that reason. That was why, as Hartman suggests, believing that Jesus was God's son and calling upon his name were the occasions on which the spirit was to be received.[14] In the new environment of God's spirit which the resurrection signaled, baptism was indeed, as Matthew 28:19 indicates, an activity and an experience which involved the father (the source of one's identity), the son (the agent of one's identity), and the holy spirit (the medium of one's identity).

The Wide Influence of the Petrine Teaching

Because the spirit in question is God's and Jesus' at one and the same time, the range of its results is extremely broad. It is as manifest as God's own creativity and as personal as an individual believer's conviction. That was skillfully brought out by Charles Gore in a study which still merits careful consideration:

> It is true that St. Luke lays stress on the wonderful signs which marked the sudden arrival of the Spirit on, or just before, the day of Pentecost, and on the similar signs which marked the first bestowal of the gift upon the Gentiles, Cornelius and his companions, and again on the twelve men who had been disciples of John the Baptist and were now

14. Hartman, *"Into the Name of the Lord Jesus,"* 140, citing Acts 8:37; 22:16.

led on into the faith of Christ.[15] And he delights
to recount the miracles of healing wrought by the
apostles. But also courage in speaking the word,
and wisdom, and faith, and large-hearted good-
ness are associated with the Spirit's presence,[16] and
He is recognized not only as the inspirer of the
prophets of old, but also as the present and personal guide and helper of individuals, and of the
assemblies of the church, in all their ways.[17]

Gore's observation is worth stressing, because there is
a persistent tendency, even in otherwise well-informed
circles, to limit unduly the place of spirit in earliest
Christianity. A reputable scholarly book refers to Acts 2,
and then to Paul's well-known caution about spiritual
gifts in 1 Corinthians 14 and goes on to state, "We hear
nothing further concerning spirit possession in the early
Church for another century..."![18]

A commonly held view has it that Christianity is not
a religion which emphasizes spirit, so that when people

---

15. Gore here is referring to the baptism in Acts 19:5–7. It would
be more accurate to say that they were followers of Jesus who had
formerly practiced immersion only as taught by John (and Jesus himself, at first). But their baptism at Paul's hands brings with it the holy
spirit.

16. He here cites Acts 4:31; 6:3, 5; 11:24.

17. Charles Gore, *The Holy Spirit and the Church,* The Reconstruc-
tion of Belief 3 (New York: Scribner's, 1924), 112.

18. Clarke Garrett, *Spirit Possession and Popular Religion: From the
Camisards to the Shakers* (Baltimore: Johns Hopkins University Press,
1987), 8.

claim that God's spirit possesses them, that is an unusual occurrence. When a movement is styled "Pentecostalist" in the current religious scene, that designation is used to characterize the group concerned as outside of the mainstream of Christianity. But the scene of Pentecost and the scene in the house of Cornelius together demonstrate that possession by God's spirit was understood to be fundamental to faith in Jesus/Yeshua, and was the principal element in the experience of baptism in the name of Jesus.

Gore also perceived that Paul was deeply influenced by this understanding of the spirit, an understanding (as we will see below) derived from the teaching of Peter regarding resurrection, baptism, and the spirit. The result is that, in Paul's letters "'in the Spirit' also means 'in Christ.'" Gore is rather tentative in regard to explaining the reason for this usage:

> We cannot speak with any confidence as to how precisely this conception was formed in St. Paul's mind. I suppose that the actual experience of the Church, before St. Paul came on the scene, had given the apostles and their companions an intense sense, as of the personal Christ now glorified in the heavens, so also of the personal Spirit, the Spirit of Jesus, guiding them from within. I suppose also that from the first they must have realized that the Holy Spirit was something more than the substitute for a now absent Christ.[19]

19. Gore, *The Holy Spirit and the Church*, 113.

When we recall Paul's confident statement that baptism is when the spirit of God's own son cries "Abba! Father!" as in the case of Jesus (so Gal. 4:6), Gore's hesitation may seem difficult to understand. Evidently, he was influenced by the notion that the spirit was somehow an unusual conception within earliest Christianity.

In fact, however, the association of the holy spirit with baptism is well attested as a principal element of earliest Christian faith. Its roots are as deep as the teaching within the circle of Peter that, since Jesus has been exalted in his resurrection, he is in a position to pour out from the spirit which had been within him on those who believe in his name (see Acts 2:30–42). Owing to Peter's influence, that conviction was passed on to Paul, who was catechized by Peter around the year 35 c.e.[20]

But beyond Paul, we also see baptism in water and the spirit portrayed in terms of a new birth in the Gospel according to John (3:1–8). That shows the extent to which the basic understanding of baptism into Jesus' name as the occasion of receiving spirit was developed further in John on the basis of the kind of teaching we also encounter in the Synoptic Gospels (under the form of Jesus' own baptism). The first letter of Peter

---

20. In regard to the relationship between Paul and Peter, see Jacob Neusner and Bruce D. Chilton, *Revelation: The Torah and the Bible:* Christianity and Judaism — The Formative Categories (Valley Forge, Pa.: Trinity Press International, 1995), 107–28. Hartman, *"Into the Name of the Lord,"* 52, 78, 84–86, also emphasizes that, in regard to baptism, Paul should be regarded as more representative than controversial.

(related only derivatively to the teaching of Peter him-self[21]) demonstrates a considerable development of the same theme. God is praised as "the God and father of our Lord, Christ Jesus" for "begetting us anew for a liv-ing hope through the resurrection of Christ Jesus from the dead" (1 Pet. 1:3). The theme of this letter, and of this passage in particular (1 Pet. 1:3–12), is that holding fast to the treasure of baptism will bring "the salvation of your souls" (1 Pet. 1:9), and that involves an awareness that what is announced to Christians was hidden even to prophets in times passed (1 Pet. 1:10–11). Now, how-ever, that is disclosed by "holy spirit sent from heaven" (1 Pet. 1:12), which is also "Christ's spirit" (1 Pet. 1:11).

That close identification between Christ's spirit and the spirit of God, characteristic of Paul's letters as well as of 1 Peter, is also vividly portrayed in the Gospel according to John. There, it is precisely the risen Jesus who bestows the holy spirit on his disciples, when they are gathered together in a closed room (20:19–22). The portrayal in this Gospel, produced at the turn of the first and second centuries,[22] is profoundly theological in its reflection of the identification of Christ and spirit. The fact that Jesus comes after the doors have been closed "on account of fear of the Jews" (20:19) estab-lishes that he comes only to the disciples, and to no one

---

21. See John H. Elliott, "Peter, First Epistle of," *Anchor Bible Dictionary* (New York: Doubleday, 1992), 5:269–78.

22. See Robert Kysar, "John, the Gospel of," *Anchor Bible Dictio-nary* (New York: Doubleday, 1992), 3:912–31.

else. Moreover, the substance of his body is quite obviously not ordinary human flesh; implicitly, John accepts the Pauline analysis that the body of the resurrected Jesus was spiritual, not carnal (see 1 Cor. 15:35–49[23]). Once in the room, limited to his own, Jesus "breathed on them and says to them, Receive holy spirit" (20:22). That statement is so laconic, its profound significance might all too easily be overlooked: Jesus personally, from his own resurrected body, breathes holy spirit on his followers.

The Spirit and the Power to Forgive

It has frequently been remarked that both the holy spirit and prophecy were widely understood to have ceased in Israel by the first century.[24] In that context, John 20:22 is startling for two reasons. First, the very presence of spirit, and indeed God's own spirit ("holy spirit"), marks

---

23. For a fuller discussion see Jacob Neusner and Bruce Chilton, *The Intellectual Foundations of Christian and Jewish Discourse: The Philosophy of Religious Argument* (London: Routledge, 1997), 70–86.

24. The passages usually cited include Tosefta Sotah 13:2f. (which speaks of Haggai, Zechariah, and Malachi as the last of the prophets), Yoma 21b in Bavli (referring to the absence of the spirit from the Second Temple), and 1 Maccabees 4:46; 9:27 (which attests that prophecy was seen as a thing of the past). For a useful review, with ample references to the primary and secondary literature, see F. W. Horn (trans. D. M. Elliott), "Holy Spirit," *The Anchor Bible Dictionary*, ed. D. N. Freedman (New York: Doubleday, 1992), 3:260–80.

the dawn of a new age. That is spelled out in Acts 2 by means of its reference to the book of Joel and is conveyed by the drama of Jesus' personal action in John. Second, the identification between Jesus and the spirit, already accomplished in Acts 2, is deeply personalized in John 20. Here, the body of the risen Jesus conveys to the disciples the power of spirit, the power to forgive. For that reason, Jesus can here say, "Just as the father sent me, so I send you" (John 20:21).

Paul had already been familiar with the idea that "by the name of our Lord Christ Jesus and by the spirit of our God" forgiveness had been granted in baptism (1 Cor. 6:11). But John takes a step beyond that common theology and finishes the scene in the closed room by having Jesus give his disciples the authority to forgive and to confirm sins (John 20:23). That is an emphatic statement in John, which contradicts the presentation in Matthew (composed around the year 80 c.e.), where Jesus — equally emphatically — delegates that authority during his ministry (to Peter in Matt. 16:19 and to his disciples in 18:18), not after his resurrection. The reason for this contradiction[25] is plainly provided in John: the spirit is given only after Jesus has been glorified:

On the last, great day of the feast [of Sukkoth, or Tabernacles, see 7:2], Jesus stood and cried out,

---

25. When John departs from the Synoptics in this manner, that is likely the result of a conscious decision; see Bruce Chilton, *Profiles of a Rabbi: Synoptic Opportunities in Reading about Jesus,* Brown Judaic Studies 177 (Atlanta: Scholars Press, 1989), 139–82.

saying, If anyone thirst, let one come to me and
drink. Who believes in me, just as Scripture says,
fountains of living water will flow out of his belly.
But he said this about the spirit, which those who
believed in him were going to receive; for there
was no spirit yet, because Jesus had not yet been
glorified. (John 7:37–39)

In his study of the Fourth Gospel, John Ashton has
clearly shown that this final statement is a governing
theme, tightly linked to the sending of the disciples in
20:21–22.[26] It is only the risen Jesus who can give the
spirit which is intimately identified with his own person and teaching, because he can function in his divine
status only as glorified.[27]

It has been argued that such an understanding of the
spirit, poured out on the disciples by and through an
explicitly divine Jesus, should be understood as the contribution of Hellenistic Christianity.[28] That argument
is based upon the books of Acts, and particularly the
figure of Stephen, viewed as "the Hellenistic ideal of
the Christian pneumatic."[29] The prophecy of Stephen

---

26. See John Ashton, *Understanding the Fourth Gospel* (Oxford:
Clarendon, 1991), 420–25.

27. That is why, once risen, Jesus can breathe creatively on his disciples just as God breathed on the first man in Genesis 2:7; see Horn,
"Holy Spirit," 266.

28. See Horn, "Holy Spirit," 268–69, especially the statement, "It
is with the Hellenists and in the Hellenistic community that we must
look for the roots of primitive Christian pneumatology" (269).

29. So ibid., 268.

against the Temple and the practices of Moses (Acts 6:14) — attributed to him by people described as false witnesses (Acts 6:13) — is the pivot of a reading according to which "the intended effect of this cultural critique was a focus on the true will of God in view of the end-time."[30] Although there is no doubt that Stephen is strongly associated with the spirit in Acts (see 6:3, 5; 7:55), such a reading of the origin of the "pneumatology" of the primitive church is unwarranted, for three principal reasons. First, Stephen's dispute is with synagogues in Jerusalem themselves drawn from the Diaspora (see Acts 6:8–15). Such Hellenists indeed spoke Greek, but many of them — such as Saul, who becomes Paul in Acts (see Acts 7:57–58) — prided themselves on a program of stamping out any perceived deviation from the Torah. Hellenism should not be directly equated with antinomianism in the study of early Judaic theologies. Second, of course, it is perilous to deduce a theology from what a person's opponents say, especially when Stephen's own speech closely calibrates attending to the holy spirit with obeying the Torah (Acts 7:51–53). The place of the Temple is obviously put in dispute by Stephen, and he and his circle represent the growing expectation of the Temple's destruction among Christians, but an antithesis between the spirit and the law should not be attributed to him. Third, association with the spirit of God is not unique to Stephen. "The bestowal is made on the whole body of the disciples," as

---

30. Ibid.

Charles Gore remarked (citing Acts 2:17f., but see also 2:4; 4:31; 9:31; 15:28),[31] and may therefore be attributed to such figures as the remaining six of the seven deacons (Acts 6:3), none of whom reportedly agrees with Stephen, as well as to Barnabas (Acts 11:24), a Levite from Cyprus who lived in the collective centered on the Temple which Peter initiated (Acts 4:36–37), and to Paul and his companions (Acts 16:7, 8; 20:22, 23).

The common denominator in all of this is not Stephen, but Peter, the preeminent figure in association with whom the spirit is given, with preaching and visions portrayed as typical results. He heads the congregation in Jerusalem and disciplines those who hold back from the collective treasure; in Peter's presence Ananias and Sapphira are struck dead for lying to the holy spirit (Acts 5:3–6, within 5:1–11). This dark side of spiritual discipline, presented among the signs and wonders of the apostles in Acts (see Acts 5:12), is in no sense incidental and is part and parcel of the ultimate authority under which Peter acts. As he himself, together with the apostles, says to the high priest later in the same chapter:

> It is necessary to submit to God rather than men. The God of our fathers raised Yeshua, whom you executed, hanging him on a tree. God exalted this man to his right hand, as precursor and savior, to give repentance to Israel and release from sins. And we are witnesses of these events, and the holy spirit

---

31. Gore, *The Holy Spirit and the Church*, 12.

which God gave to those who submit to him. (Acts 5:29b–32)

Vision, testimony (in whatever language is necessary), and signs of power are the marks of the apostles because the holy spirit joins in their witness. That is central to the theology of Peter's circle as it is portrayed in Acts. Just that spirit, within the ministry of Peter, guides him by vision and attests the propriety of baptism by verbal testimony as he proceeds to include non-Jews (see Acts 10:44–48, discussed above).

History and Spirit and Resurrection

Acts may be said to be the story of the outward moving impact of the spirit from its center in Jerusalem. Once the inclusion of non-Jews is accepted, those who are associated with Paul and Barnabas in Antioch (named as Symeon called Niger, Lucius of Cyrene, and Manaen, an associate of Herod Antipas[32]), as well as those apostles themselves, are said to be directed by the spirit (Acts 13:1–4; 16:6–10; 20:28). Paul becomes the principal agent of baptism and the spirit, once the field of mission is far from Antioch, and it is from his perspec-

---

32. Within the communities of the first century which heard Luke and Acts read, the irony that the movement in Antioch included an associate of the person responsible for Yohanan's execution (Luke 3:18–20; 9:7–9), and involved in Yeshua's execution (Luke 23:6–12) was no doubt appreciated.

tive that the story of Apollos's ministry in Ephesus and Corinth is told (Acts 18:24–19:7). Apollos teaches only what is called the baptism of John, although Priscilla and Aquila correct him. But the definitive correction occurs when Paul comes to Ephesus, and those who had been baptized into John's baptism are now baptized into Jesus' name and receive the holy spirit when Paul lays his hands on them.[33]

Jerome Murphy-O'Connor has suggested that the reason for distinctive practices of baptism within primitive Christianity was that some followers of Jesus continued his practice while he was a disciple of John's, while most understood baptism as redefined by those who knew "the Risen Lord."[34] That distinction is crucial for an understanding of the literary program of Acts and of the practice of baptism after the resurrection of Jesus. The spirit, as released in baptism into the name of Jesus, is what distinguishes the practice of the church from the practice of Jesus, and what explains why the movement which had defined itself during Jesus' life by desisting from baptism now made baptism its emblem. The con-

---

33. Because Apollos was a Hellenist, a Jew from the Greek-speaking Diaspora (and Alexandria, at that; Acts 18:24), the theory that the "pneumatology" of the New Testament is a general product of Christian Hellenism is further vitiated.

34. See Jerome Murphy-O'Connor, "John the Baptist and Jesus: History and Hypotheses," *New Testament Studies* 36 (1990): 367–68. By way of support, the implicit criticism of Philip's practice of immersion (Acts 8:12–17) might also be mentioned. It is notable that, when Philip next baptizes (Acts 8:26–40), the spirit plays an important role in the narrative.

trast the risen Jesus makes in Acts is instructive: "John indeed baptized with water, while you will be baptized in holy spirit" (Acts 1:5). What is marked here is not only a periodization in time, of the resurrection as the caesura between immersing for purity and baptizing into Jesus' name; a change in the actual medium of baptism is also marked. The medium in John's immersion was water, because the issue was purification; the medium of baptism into the name of Jesus is spirit, because the issue is the empowerment which that spirit brings. As the risen Jesus goes on to say, "But you will receive power when the holy spirit has come upon you, and you will become my witnesses both in Jerusalem and all Judaea and Samaria, even to the end of the earth" (Acts 1:8). That, of course, articulates a major theme within the Gospel according to Luke and within Acts. At the same time, it expresses the theology of God's spirit which explains the activity of Peter after the resurrection.

The conviction that God's spirit could bring about resurrection is already attested in the book of Ezekiel, when, in a famous vision, the LORD states he will cause spirit to enter dry bones in order to make them live (Ezek. 37:5). That wording is recalled in the Eighteen Benedictions, an ancient prayer of the synagogue whose roots reach into the first century.[35] The association of spirit and being raised from the dead was therefore well attested by the time of Jesus' resurrection. Within the

---

35. See Horn, "Holy Spirit," 267; he there cites additional evidence.

circle of Peter, as we have seen on the evidence of Acts, that association was the very foundation of the life of the church, and the Petrine experience and teaching concerning God's spirit and its availability by baptism into the name of Jesus became a fundamental characteristic of Christianity.

Indeed, even the link between resurrection and water in Peter's theology is easier to understand on the basis of early Judaic theology. The Eighteen Benedictions allude not only to Ezekiel, but to Isaiah. The reference in Isaiah 26:19 to God's "dew of light" there was widely understood to signify how he would raise the dead. This is clearly brought out in the Aramaic Targum of Isaiah (26:19):

> *You are he who brings a*live the dead, *you* ra*ise the bones of their* bodies. *All who were thrown in the* dust *will live* and sing *before you!* For your dew is a dew of light *for those who perform your law,* and *the wicked to whom you have given might, and they transgressed against your Memra,* you will *hand over to Gehenna.*[36]

Just as the Eighteen Benedictions allude to both Ezekiel 37:5 and Isaiah 26:19, so here, in the Aramaic rendition of Isaiah 26:19, the "bones" of Ezekiel 37 make their appearance. Spirit, God's luminous "dew," and resurrection

---

36. As in my translation and commentary of the Targum, departures from the Hebrew text are rendered in italics; see Bruce Chilton, *The Isaiah Targum: Introduction, Translation, Apparatus, and Notes,* Aramaic Bible 11 (Wilmington: Glazier; Edinburgh: Clark, 1987).

were already linked in the eschatology of early Judaism and formed a vital precedent of Peter's experience of the resurrection of Jesus.

Although Simon Peter is clearly portrayed as the principal witness of Jesus' resurrection within the New Testament (see Luke 24:34 and 1 Cor. 15:5), there is only one narrative in the canon which portrays his experience of the risen Jesus. John 21 is widely agreed to be an addendum to the Fourth Gospel, and only derivatively related to Peter,[37] and yet its utility for understanding the Petrine theology of resurrection may not be discounted. Here, Peter and six other disciples are fishing on the sea of Galilee, and Jesus appears on the shore unrecognized, asking if they have anything to eat. They have not caught anything all night, but at Jesus' command they cast their net and catch more fish than they can pull up.[38] The disciple whom Jesus loves recognizes Jesus and informs Peter who the stranger is. Peter leaps into the water and swims to shore, followed by the others in the boat. Jesus, whose identity none dares to ask, directs the preparation of breakfast from the 153

---

37. See Pierre Benoit, *Passion et résurrection du Seigneur* (Paris: Cerf, 1985), 327–53; Ashton, *Understanding the Fourth Gospel,* 382.

38. The obvious comparison is with Luke 5:4–11, where a miraculous catch of fish initiates Simon Peter's discipleship. It is frequently been suggested that Luke transposes a scene of resurrection from its original position (which John gives). In fact, any transposition is likely to have been the other way around. John delays both the apostolic forgiveness of sins (John 20:23) and baptized discipleship (John 21) until after Jesus' glorification and his breathing of the spirit on his followers.

large fish which were caught. Finally, Peter himself is commissioned to shepherd the flock of Jesus.

Although this third appearance of the risen Jesus in John is the only appearance which features Peter,[39] the allusions to baptism and the direction of the church make it clear that it is far from the sort of tradition which would have been formed in any immediate proximity to Peter's experience. Still, one feature stands out. As in the story of what happened near and at Emmaus (which holds the place of an appearance to Peter in Luke 24:13–35), Jesus is not immediately known; his identity is a matter of inference (see John 21:7, 12, and Luke 24:16, 31). This, of course, is just the direction which all of the Gospels are *not* headed in by their structuring of traditions. They anticipate an instantly recognizable Jesus, fully continuous with the man who was buried: that is the point of the story of the empty tomb in all four Gospels. The earlier Petrine understanding of resurrection allows for a discontinuity between the risen Jesus and Jesus prior to his death, just as it makes room for the influence of the holy spirit on those who experience Jesus as alive after his execution.

---

39. It has been argued that the *Gospel of Peter* represents a more primitive tradition, but the fact is that the text incorporates elements from the canonical Gospels. It appears to be a pastiche, much in the vein of the longer ending of Mark. See James H. Charlesworth and Craig A. Evans, "Jesus in the Agrapha and Apocryphal Gospels," *Studying the Historical Jesus: Evaluations of the State of Current Research,* New Testament Tools and Studies 19, ed. B. Chilton and C. A. Evans (Leiden: Brill, 1994), 503–14.

Just as Peter's leaping into the water in John 21 is redolent of baptism into the name of Jesus, so is this moment the completion of the baptismal imagery articulated early in the Gospel. In his nocturnal discussion with Rabbi Nicodemus, Jesus says, "Unless one is born from water and spirit, one cannot enter into the kingdom of God" (John 3:5). By the Johannine definition, that obvious prophecy of baptism cannot be realized during Jesus' life, but only after Jesus' glorification, when spirit becomes available (see John 7:37–39 and the discussion above). Now that Jesus has breathed the spirit on his followers (so John 20:22), the spirit has been released, and such a new birth is possible. John 21 attests the connection among spirit, baptism, and resurrection within the circle of Peter, even as it completes the promise of Jesus in John 3:5.[40]

Fortunately, there is an additional confirmation of the Petrine theology of resurrection and spirit. Paul, who had himself studied with Peter (see Gal. 1:18), not only refers to Peter as the principal witness of the resurrection (1 Cor. 15:5), but also opens his letter to the Romans with what is widely agreed to be a primitive statement of Jesus' identity:

> Paul, Jesus Christ's slave, called an apostle — separated for God's message, which he declare beforehand through his prophets in holy scriptures

---

40. For this reason, the consensus that John 21 did not originally belong to the Gospel is seriously to be questioned.

concerning his son, come from David's seed according to flesh, designated God's son in power according to spirit of sanctity, by resurrection of the dead, Christ Jesus our Lord. (Rom. 1:1–4)

Jesus' resurrection and Jesus' designation as God's son together are attested and enabled by the spirit of God. That is a founding principle of Christianity.

Paul, for all the controversy he occasioned, is a representative teacher of the primitive church when it concerns the spirit of God. He understands that the spirit of sonship which raised Jesus from the dead is also available to Jesus' followers in baptism:

For as many as are led by God's spirit, they are God's sons. Because you did not receive a spirit of slavery again, for fear, but you received a spirit of sonship, by which we cried out, Abba, Father! The spirit itself testified with our spirit that we are God's children. (Rom. 8:14–16)

For Paul, as for the earliest Christians of the Petrine tradition, creation itself longed for the fulfillment of God's spirit, because God was making the world anew with a new people (see Rom. 8:22–23), and it had begun with the resurrection of his own son.

What had begun with the immersion of Yohanan and his disciple Yeshua, practiced for the purpose of purification, had become something new and distinctive and — within the practice of Christian faith — absolutely fundamental. Baptism now was into Jesus' name for the reception of the holy spirit. God's presence was so intimate and commanding, what happened amounted to a "new creation" (so Paul in Gal. 6:15–16). Moreover, the principle of contagious, healing purity — which had emerged in Yeshua's practice (see chap. 3, pp. 71–78) — was consciously taken up in the life of the church after the resurrection. Nowhere is that principle more clearly articulated than in the practice of laying on hands. The articulation takes place in two steps.

First, the remembrance of the Gospels insists upon that characteristic in the activity of Yeshua: in purifying (so the story of the leper, Matt. 8:3; Mark 1:41; Luke 5:13), in healing (so the story of Peter's mother-in-law, Matt. 8:15; Mark 1:31), and raising from death (so the story of Yair's daughter, Matt. 9:18, 25; Mark 5:23, 41; Luke 8:54). Other stories — Mark's deaf mute (7:32), blind man (8:23, 25), and possessed boy (9:27); Luke's crippled woman (13:13) and servant of the high priest (22:51) — as well as a telling summary of Yeshua's typical acts (Mark 6:5) make it plain that healing was the overarching category which linked these restorations into the community of Israel.[41] But the characteristic is so strong, touching in itself becomes the emblem of acceptance by Yeshua (see the story of the children, Matt. 19:13–15; Mark 10:13–16; Luke 18:15–17).

---

41. Because that was the overarching category, touch — even touching Yeshua's garment — can be used to achieve healing; see the story of the woman with a hemorrhage (Matt. 9:20–21; Mark 5:27–28; Luke 8:44).

That leads to the second step in the articulation. The followers of Yeshua act by laying on hands principally to heal at first, as in the case of Peter with John and the lame man in the Temple (Acts 3:7). But the apostolic church is clear that this is a matter of God himself "stretching forth a hand so that healing and signs and powers are done by the name of your holy child Yeshua" (Acts 4:30). Just as healing had been possible in the case of Yeshua because the spirit of God was identified with him in an unprecedented way, so healing among the apostles is occasioned by the unprecedented outpouring of that spirit after the resurrection. Peter's speech in the house of Cornelius is again precisely instructive of the ideology of the apostolic church in this case: God is said to have anointed Jesus "by the holy spirit and power" (Acts 10:38), and then that same spirit "fell upon all those hearing the word" of Jesus' resurrection (10:44). The holy spirit, the same spirit initially active in the case of Jesus, becomes contagiously available from the apostles.

Just as the holy spirit is understood to be available by means of the apostles, so the range of its activity is every bit as broad — and indeed broader — than the example of Jesus would lead one to expect. Laying on of hands, associated with the holy spirit, designates the seven deacons who have special responsibilities for the Greek-speaking disciples in Jerusalem (Acts 6:6), as well as Barnabas and Saul as delegates of the church in Antioch (13:2–3). That gesture is unequivocally associated with the coming of the spirit when Peter and John travel to Samaria in order to assure that those baptized into Yeshua's name by Philip should also receive the holy spirit (Acts 8:17–19). That story, together with the much discussed laying on of hands on Apollos's disciples (Acts 19:6), establishes that the circle of Peter was especially responsible for primitive Christian teaching in regard to the spirit, and that Paul was in that sense a member of the Petrine circle. By the time of Hebrews, baptism and laying on of hands were associated closely, because they referred to a commonly accepted pairing of immersion into Jesus' name and reception of the spirit of God (Heb. 6:2).

But however broad and generally available the holy spirit in apostolic baptism was understood to be, its miraculous power as coming from God is underscored in Acts. By laying on hands Ananias heals Paul (Acts 9:17–18), Paul himself heals on the way to Rome (Acts 28:8), Peter raises "Tabitha" (Acts 9:41) in a manner which recalls Yeshua's raising of the young woman (*talitha*) who was Yair's daughter, all because the creative power of God was at work. To be immersed into Jesus' name was also to be drenched with the outpouring of God's spirit and the social and natural and supernatural changes in the understanding of purity which that involved.

Biblical Index

General Index